The Essential Guide to Buying and Selling Homes

Insights from America's Top Agents and Loan Officers

Kathy May-Martin
Robin Lemon
Gus Pasquale
Christine Rich
Frank Bennett
Josh Vernon
Jamey Reynolds
Brad Roche
Jason Perlow
Troy Olson

Table of Contents

Introduction

According to the National Association of REALTORS® there are over 1.3 million real estate agent or broker members in the United States. The publisher selected seven top real estate agents and brokers from around the county to contribute to this book. Mortgage lenders are a critical component of most real estate transactions. The publisher also selected three top mortgage company executives and loan officer to contribute to the book to describe lending strategies for successful real estate transactions.

Each of the contributors has a high volume of completed transactions, is highly rated by their clients, and is an advocate for their clients' success. The contributors are spread out geographically across the United States. Each contributor has provided their insights for home buyers and/or sellers in their respective area and with strategies that can work anywhere in the country. We hope that this book will become a useful reference for consumers interested in buying or selling homes around the United States.

NMG Publishing

The Keys to Success When Selling Your Home

Kathy May-Martin

Introduction

Kathy May-Martin has been helping buyers and sellers with their real estate transactions in the greater Knoxville, Tennessee area for over 27 years. She works with sellers in all walks of life, whether they are selling their first home and upscaling or are retirees transitioning to a new lifestyle. Kathy has extensive experience in all aspects of real estate in Knoxville and the surrounding communities and she has been ranked numerous times among the top 1% of all Coldwell Banker agents nationally.

In this chapter, Kathy provides insight about the most important factors for selling your home for the most money and in the shortest time.

Clarifying Your Objectives

The client/agent relationship usually starts with an introductory meeting or interview. During this first meeting, it's important to clarify your objectives to your agent so both of you are on the same page with respect to your needs and expectations. Your reasons for selling and the timing of the sale are some key discussion points. Does your preference for timing align with market realities? Market conditions and seasonality factors come into play when selecting the best time to sell and how long it's likely to take to find a buyer.

Pricing Your Home for the Market

Value and the ultimate sales price are set by the market. It's what a willing buyer will pay for your home. The Internet has an abundance of information and homeowners can see estimates of home value online from a variety of sites. They can also find prices of homes that have sold in their neighborhood or surrounding areas. Armed with this information as well as tax assessments, and maybe an appraisal for refinancing from a few years back, many homeowners prejudge the market value of their home. It's extremely useful to get an informed opinion on your home's value from an experienced and trusted agent that knows your local market to ensure that your expectations are not too low or out of line with market realties.

Online market estimates are rarely correct. They are not a substitute for an experienced real estate agent who can accurately do an analysis and determine a price range that the home is likely to sell for. Every property is unique and the online pricing estimators don't really know how your home compares to other homes in the area except for some statistical indicators that are only part of the equation.

A thorough analysis of market value considers many factors. The current level of supply and demand for similar properties gives us some indications of market itself and how long it is typically taking to sell aa home. We will be comparing your home to similar homes that have sold in the last three to six months as well as homes that are currently on the market, which are your immediate competition for a buyer. It's important to analyze the differences between your home and the homes that have sold and adjust for differences that account for more or less value. We will be comparing size of the homes, location, age, condition, lot size, view, quality of construction, upgrades, level of finishes, amenities in the area, how long each home was on the market, how long since sold, and other factors in making our comparative analysis. We focus on comparing homes that are as close in location and as similar as possible to your home. As an example, if your home is on a lake, we will compare to other lake properties. If your home is a smaller ranch-style home in an older subdivision, we will compare to other ranch-style homes in similar age developments. Depending on the amount of sales in the recent few months we may need to go outside from your immediate location to find enough similar homes to compare.

Although some agents typically provide one number as an estimated value, I prefer to establish a market value price range, because the sales price depends on seller motivations. If the home needs to be sold quickly, maybe within 30 days because of a job transfer, it may be appropriate to list at the lower end of the estimated price range. If you're not in a hurry and want to wait for the highest possible price, you may decide to list at the higher end of the range.

Setting an appropriate listing price not only reduces the time on market but can also generate the highest price for your home. A common mistake is to set an unrealistically high listing price, expecting that potential buyers will want to negotiate the price down. The thought is that setting a high price gives you plenty of room to negotiate and you will be able to achieve a higher final sale price. Another misconception is that you can always drop the price later if the home isn't getting offers. Unfortunately, this philosophy sets sellers up for disappointment. Most buyers today are looking for homes online and they set up alerts for new listings based on price ranges and the most active time for buyer interest is right after a home is listed. If your home is priced too high, buyers might not see it because it's not priced within their range. Even if you drop the price later, they might not notice since it's not shown as a new listing. If your home is not attracting offers, it just languishes on the market and now even if you drop the price, buyers just wonder what is wrong with the home, and you may be stuck with low-ball offers. Setting the listing price within the market value range up front provides the best opportunity for achieving the highest price and selling in the fastest time.

Preparing Your Home for Sale

You only get one chance to make a first impression and it's important that your property presents well if you want to sell it. Exterior appearance is even more important now as buyers are looking online, and they may drive by your home to see what it looks like. If the exterior doesn't present well, we're probably not going to get them through the front door.

The exterior needs to be in good condition and have a clean appearance. Any drainage problems should be addressed. Something that's often overlooked are tree limbs overhanging the house which will cause the gutters to fill with leaves. Anything that needs repair should be fixed, because the issues will come up in the inspection report and some buyers usually imagine repairs being a lot more expensive than if the seller handled them. Focus on what buyers will see as they drive into your driveway and walk up to the front door. The walkways should be power washed and the landscaping well-manicured. In the few seconds that the agent is getting the key, buyers are looking around at the condition of everything around the door. Chipped paint on porch railings or trim, issues with the door hardware, or visible cobwebs will not present a good impression right from the start.

Of course, the interior needs to be spotless and appliances and equipment should all be in good working condition. Pay attention to the paint and repaint or touch up walls and trim that show evidence of paint chipping. I walk room-by-room through the home and provide a list of points that should be addressed. Typically, most suggestions are simple and don't involve much investment. If you have noticeably dated flooring and appliances, that can be a concern and may limit your ability to attract an offer.

Space is something that buyers are always concerned about so it's critical to make your home appear as open and spacious as possible so buyers can visualize their furnishings and personal items fitting in the home. Kitchens are very important, so make sure the counter tops, cabinets, and pantry are uncluttered. Adequate closet space is almost always a concern, so pack away some of your clothes so closets can be displayed with plenty of extra space. In general, you should pack up most of your personal decorative items, so walls and shelves are not filled. Too much furniture will make your home crowded and look smaller. Sometimes I will recommend removing some furniture, keeping the main items. You will be packing and moving anyway, so it's better to pack up what is not needed while your home is on the market. Garages are also important because people want to see there is room for cars, tools, and hobbies. The best solution is to have a moving sale or rent a storage space or POD, so you are not just cluttering the garage or another room with the packed items.

Some homeowners prefer having a professional stager work with them to get their home prepared. Professional staging makes a large difference in presentation that will be apparent in photos that will be used online to catch buyers' attention and get them to into the home. It also carries over in making a great impression as buyers are visiting the home.

It's critical to make sure your home presents well and issues are handled up front. Your competition has probably already paid attention to the details and if your home is not shining like the others on the market, buyers will stop looking. Like being overpriced, if you home sits on the market, buyers are more likely to bypass it because they believe something must be wrong with the home.

Presenting Your Home to the Market

With most buyers searching for homes online, high quality photography is essential to tell the story of your home and to attractively display the best features. After your home has been thoroughly cleaned, prepared, and decluttered, we will bring in a professional photographer to capture the beauty of the home and its surroundings. Wide-angle lenses should be used to accurately present the main rooms, such as the kitchen and master bedroom as well as the exterior. Drone photography is very useful to show the home in its setting, especially when there is a view, or if the home is on a lake. Attractive pictures make a big difference in grabbing the attention of online viewers and we just have a few seconds to capture their attention.

While most home listings provide an outline description of the property, I prefer to develop a more comprehensive description that will identify all the important features, provide an accurate presentation of the home, and give buyers additional reasons to schedule a showing. I oftentimes ask the sellers to make a list of what was important to them when they purchased the home and what they think are the most attractive aspects of the home and the location. This helps me write a compelling description.

I want to make it as easy as possible for buyers to get accurate information about the home and especially if they are viewing a home with their buyer's agent and I am not present at a showing. I display as much information as possible along with a picture brochure and property description for buyers to take with them so they can view again later. When buyers are visiting several properties in a day, they tend to confuse aspects of homes they have seen.

Open houses, especially for brokers and agents to preview the home, is another strategy I often use to build excitement as the home is hitting the market. Other agents may have clients that our listing is suitable for, so this is another way to get exposure.

Showings

The goals of our marketing and exposure is to get potential buyers into the home, so we want to make the most of every showing. It's important to keep your home as clean and uncluttered as possible—in show-ready condition. Keep the temperature set to a comfortable setting. Make sure all the lights are working and light bulbs are installed.

Although we like to schedule showings with some notice, being flexible with access on short notice, creates a better chance of selling the home in a short period of time. Sometimes buyers' schedules dictate when your home needs to be shown. Out of town buyers may have a very short time in the area to look at homes and if you can't work within their schedule, you may have lost an opportunity for a sale.

Homeowners should always be away from the home during showings. Buyers don't feel comfortable looking through the home and being objective if the homeowner is present. If they aren't objective and don't openly express their concerns, their agent doesn't have the opportunity to overcome any objections.

Negotiating the Agreement

Your home is on the market and is attracting offers, but how do you decide which offer is the best deal for you? Price isn't the only important factor. The buyer's ability to obtain financing is critical and I don't recommend considering any offer that is not accompanied with a preapproval letter from a reliable lender. Even with a preapproval letter, we need to make sure the home, itself, conforms to the financing standards for the loan type. Not all homes will meet the financing standards for FHA, VA, or rural development loans.

We critically review any contingencies the buyer is requesting over the typical ones: home inspection, financing, and appraisal. Even with a preapproval letter, a financing contingency will usually be included in the contract. If there are multiple offers, we will help you review the various terms and conditions, as well as the price, to make an educated comparison.

We are basically taking the home off the market when you sign an agreement, so we want to minimize the risk of the sale not closing by being careful with complicating contingencies. Even though we still have the home listed, it will show as sale pending status. Traffic drops off significantly after a home is shown as "pending" because buyers don't want to waste their time looking at a home that's already under contract. If a buyer needs to sell an existing home to be able to close on your home, you have little control, so it's a big risk.

We'll want to know how long the buyer's house has been on the market, or is it under contract?

If the home has been on the market for a while and there is only one offer, you may need to be a bit more flexible on the price and the terms and conditions. We're going to review how long it's been on the market and if there were previous offers. We'll also look at how many showings we've had as well as feedback from the showings? Based on the facts, we will evaluate the likelihood of receiving another offer or a better offer.

Getting to the Closing

The contract is signed, but we still need to navigate the rest of the way through to the closing. This is an emotional time for both the buyers and the sellers, and there are potential obstacles that can impede the path to the closing. The first hurdle is getting through the home inspection. I discussed earlier about the importance of making sure the home and its systems are in good condition before we list the home. If we have done a good job in addressing problems up front, this is not likely to much of an issue, but it's the inspector's job to complete a very thorough inspection to advise the buyer of the home's condition, and most inspections have some findings. Frequently buyers will want the sellers to address some of the issues. Depending on the extent of the issues and the cost to remedy, the seller needs to decide how to address requests to make repairs. At the purchase price we have accepted, is it worth making the repairs? You need to consider that inspection findings will likely come back up again if we don't agree to remedy the issues and the buyers back out of the agreement.

Another potential hurdle is the appraisal. Most agreements have a contingency for the home appraising for at least the agreed purchase price and lenders require that the appraisal come in at or above the purchase price. Before listing, we reviewed comps and our assessment of market value should have been an accurate estimate. There are still times when an appraisal comes in low. This can be a very difficult situation for the parties involved. In order to get to the closing table, all parties involved need to find a reasonable compromise or lose the deal.

Compliance to timelines set forth in the agreement is critical. I work with my clients and other parties to the contract to make sure we stay on schedule and get to the closing. Experience is critical and I work to make get to the closing as seamlessly as possible.

Selecting an Agent

A house is a significant financial asset, so most homeowners want to make sure an experienced and trustworthy agent is handling the sale process for them. You want to get the sense that your agent will always be looking out for your best interests.

Experience level, particularly in the number of successful home sales the agent has handled is one factor to consider. Knowledge of the specific market where your home is located is important. Buyers are often moving into the area from out of town, so we're not just selling a home, we're also selling the community. Experience level should also give you the confidence that the agent can provide advice on countering offers and lead the negotiations that are inevitably a part of every sale.

As you are evaluating agents, look at their websites. Are they current and up to date on technology? Look at how agents are marketing their listings. Do they have the advertising budget and capabilities to get your home the maximum exposure, so you have the best opportunity for your home to be sold in a reasonable time and for the highest price.?

Communication style is important for most people, so find out who you will be communicating with and how during your home sale transaction. As an example, some agents will have you communicating with several different people during certain phases of the process. I prefer to handle all communications with my clients directly. I have assistants that work in the background handling computer and administrative work, so I can focus on the selling and communication with my sellers.

What Clients Are Saying

"Kathy is an excellent realtor who is responsive, professional and very helpful. She knows her stuff, has been in the business a long time, and also understands the stresses of selling a house. She will do her best for you."

--Leslie H.

"Kathy May-Martin was a consummate professional throughout the sale of our home. Her honesty, integrity, wisdom and experience coupled with a genuine caring for helping us sell our home make her first among real estate professionals. We would not hesitate to recommend Kathy to anyone in need of a truly competent and efficient real estate professional."

--Rebecca P.

"Kathy helped my wife and I purchase our first home 15 years ago. Since then, we've sold three houses and Kathy has been our agent every time. We have never considered hiring anyone else to be our agent. She has always been second to none. Each time has been a wonderful experience, without any frustrations. She is professional, knowledgeable, patient, and has great communication skills. Without any doubt, we highly recommend her."

--Ryan W.

"Kathy May-Martin was a joy to work with. She made selling our lake home as stress-free as it could possibly be. She knows her market and provided excellent counsel on pricing, staging and

negotiating. Her honesty and straightforward manner were much appreciated. When she told us our house would not stay on the market long she was right! I highly recommend her."

--Maria S.

"Kathy May-Martin personally handled the selling of our home from the initial walk through to closing. Her spot-on advice for staging our home was certainly one component of our quick sale. Ms. May-Martin was always available to answer questions or handle any needs for us as we were 500 miles away while the home was on the market. She was very helpful in the negotiation process and during closing. Feedback from prospective buyers was emailed in a timely fashion. I would highly recommend Kathy May-Martin for your real estate needs."

--Jan K.

"Kathy is pro-active, very responsive, and knowledgeable. She if flexible and responded to calls and emails day or night, on the weekends and even while on vacation. We enjoyed working with her and would highly recommend her if you are buying or selling a home."

--Brenda H.

About Kathy May-Martin

Kathy May-Martin is the managing broker for the Coldwell Banker Jim Henry & Associates office in Kingston, Tennessee. She has over 27 years of experience helping buyers and sellers with their real estate transactions in the greater Knoxville area. Kathy has extensive knowledge in all facets of real estate in Knoxville and surrounding areas. She has been ranked numerous times in the top 1% of all Coldwell Banker agents nationally.

Kathy has won numerous awards for sales excellence including:

- Coldwell Banker Office Manager's Award for Excellence 2003

- Coldwell Banker International Premier 2016, 2017, 2018

- Coldwell Banker President's Circle 2001, 2002, 2003, 2004, 2011, 2012

- Colwell Banker International President's Elite 2014, 2015

She also contributes her time to local community organizations including:

- Chairman of Roane County Chamber of Commerce 2008

- Roane County Chamber of Commerce Board of Directors 2005-2008, 2012-2019

- Roane Alliance Roan County Certified Economic Developer 2004

- Fort Sanders Foundation Board 2017, 2018, 2019

- Healthcare Leadership Graduate 2018

For more information about Kathy May-Martin, visit https://www.KathyMayMartin.com.

Buying and Selling Your Metro Atlanta Area Home

Robin Lemon

Introduction

Robin Lemon and her family lived in Las Vegas where she owned and operated a successful business. After selling the business, she got started in the real estate industry working with housing developers. She helped them fund their projects with HUD grants and tax funds working as an analyst for the City of Las Vegas. She enjoyed working with real estate and after she and her husband moved to Georgia in 2005, Robin got her real estate license so she could work on the other side of the table representing buyers and sellers.

Robin rapidly developed an award-winning real estate team helping buyers and sellers in the northern suburbs of the Atlanta Metro area. She is affiliated with Keller Williams in Roswell, Georgia. About 75% of Robin's clients are repeat customers or referral-based.

In this chapter, Robin provides insights for buyers and sellers in the Metro Atlanta area.

Selling Your Atlanta Area Home

<u>Clarifying Objectives and Understanding the Market</u>

When first meeting with homeowners interested in selling their home, we have them talk about their reasons for selling and we discuss their expectations for the selling process. Are there specific circumstances that dictate timing of the sale? They generally have an idea about the price they expect to sell for, but is it realistic in the current market? The best results for the seller are achieved when we have good communication and a mutual understanding on objectives and expectations. In that way we can be prepared to match or exceed our clients' expectations within the relationship.

During our first meeting we discuss prevailing market conditions and the implications for the time to sell and the sales strategy. National trends, economic conditions, and interest rates influence the real estate market in general, but real estate is a very localized market. We generally talk about being in either a seller's market or a buyer's market and the market situation can vary by specific location or neighborhood. We typically consider the market to be balanced when there is about a six-month supply of houses for sale. If there is more than six months of inventory, it is considered a buyer's market and buyers have more homes to choose from and usually hold a stronger negotiating position. With less than six months of supply, it's considered a seller's market and sellers typically are in a better position. Atlanta has been a relatively stable market without drastic swings in value. Even though we have experienced a seller's market in recent years, buyers are not bidding up prices substantially and sellers need to make sure their homes are well presented to attract buyers' attention. The market condition also varies by price point. While we may be in a seller's market for prices up to $500 thousand, and a transitional market between $500 – $700 thousand, homes priced near and above $1 million are usually in a buyer's market as there are fewer buyers able to afford these properties. That's important to understand when setting expectations for selling your home within a high price range.

Factors That Influence Maximizing the Sales Price

Some people believe that setting a high listing price (to "just see what kind of action it brings"), may leave them room to drop the price if it doesn't sell or negotiate with buyers that are looking for a discount. The reality is that a home should be listed very close to the anticipated market price. First, buyers are usually looking in specific price points and if your home is priced too high, they are likely to miss even seeing the listing. Additionally, buyers are comparing your home to others they see, and an unrealistic listing price dramatically reduces the number of buyers that will even request a showing. If the home lingers on the market, then buyers and their agents wonder what is wrong with the home. Now you need to reduce the price and that's another red flag. Often, a seller trying to chase the market ends up losing the gamble, and in the end, must settle for a lower price than if the home were priced competitively from the start.

Accurately estimating market value is a skill that is developed with experience. Yes, there are online estimating tools, but they are rarely accurate. The online tools are based on statistical information about other homes that have sold in the same general area. They compare price per square foot, number of rooms, and similar statistical data, but other key factors of value like the condition of the property, views, level of finishes, upgrades, and landscaping features are not part of their algorithms.

Our market analysis is focused on comparing several of the most similar homes that have recently sold in the same or nearby neighborhoods. We review similar competing homes currently for sale. Statistical factors are relevant as a baseline, but we critically review other characteristics. Condition of each property is reviewed including ages of the primary systems and roof type and age. We also evaluate the view, detail location, level of finishes, and upgrades. We review seller disclosures and listing details for the other properties being compared and study the photos to compare competing properties with your home. Historical experience in the local market, comparing hundreds of homes and the value influencers, is critical to an accurate market value estimate. Armed with a clear estimate of value, we can develop a pricing strategy that will position a home to sell in the fastest time and at the highest price point.

Some homes are well maintained and don't need much effort to get them prepared for sale. Often, some maintenance has been neglected or issues have gone unnoticed due to familiarity with living in the home. When selling a used car, it needs to be detailed first if you expect top dollar. It's the same when selling a home. We walk through the home and make a list of priorities for our sellers. We review the list and their budget together and we help them decide which items to address to maximize the net profit on the sale.

Appliances, fixtures, and the primary home systems should be in good working condition. Any evidence of wood rot should be repaired. Updating the paint can dramatically freshen up the home. Refinishing and staining hardwood floors can be expensive, but the addition of builder grade carpet can make the home more appealing, sometimes at a lower cost. Of course, your home needs to be thoroughly cleaned and organized. Look at the exterior, especially the front of the home where buyers will be walking up to your front door. Power wash the walks and driveway if there are any stains. The house exterior can usually benefit from a power wash as well to remove dirt and stains.

We're finding that the largest group among first time

homebuyers in recent years are around their mid-thirties. They are used to watching home improvement shows on TV and expect to see more updates and more value in what they are paying for in a home. On the other hand, they are less likely to know how to make repairs and haven't worked with contractors or gotten bids or estimates. Condition and presentation are critical, and when buyers walk through a home that needs repairs or updates, they are ticking off anticipated costs that are probably going to be inflated beyond realistic costs. They will expect a deep discount and a home that is not in good condition and being sold "as is" will get "foreclosure" type of offers. Often, an investment of $5,000 to $8,000 for interior and exterior painting and perhaps new carpeting can yield a far better return than just selling "as is."

As we move up in price range to luxury properties, buyers' expectations are significantly higher and it's even more important to make your home stand out as an exceptional property. Professionally staging your luxury home can make a big difference in presentation. Studies have shown that 88% of staged homes sell at or above list price and on average they sell seven times faster. The cost of staging is usually less than 1% of the list price and can be worked into the price to accommodate the additional expense.

Like most areas of the country, spring is the most active time for home selling activity in the Atlanta area. There's more demand in the spring, but also more competition for sales, and therefore a greater need to get the home ready to be the "beauty contest winner." Conversely, if you go on the market in the fall or winter, there is less competition and you can expect serious buyers with realistic expectations at those times.

<u>Negotiating the Best Deal</u>

Your home is filled with memories and selling it is an emotional process. You have decided to sell, and we encourage you to consider the home now as a product. Our job is to move the product for the highest price so you can obtain something of greater value. As your agent, we bring value to the transaction by understanding your motivation and working as a buffer with the buyer to reduce emotional tensions. We've found that communication of important points to the buyer's agent before preparation of an offer can maximize the initial offer and reduce the negotiation cycle. We also like to get as much information from the buyer's agent about what's most important to the buyer. Sometimes it's paying for certain closing costs on their behalf or a home warranty or other incentive. In this way we can try to work the extra value into the sales price and get to a win-win deal for both parties.

Once a purchase contract is signed, we still need to navigate the transaction all the way to closing. Getting past the home inspection is one of the hurdles and we advise on addressing issues that arise. An often-overlooked obstacle is the appraisal that will be ordered by the buyer's lender. We're very confident about the work we have done in our original assessment of market value and want to do everything possible to ensure the appraiser will recognize at least the same value in the home. We show up while the appraiser is at our client's home and provide information about the comparables we used along with feature differences used to substantiate the value analysis. This reinforces the work we have already done and sometimes makes the difference on a deal making it to the closing.

Selling your home can be an extremely stressful time. Having an experienced agent on your side will minimize the stress and help you achieve your objectives and maximize the value of your property.

Buying Your Atlanta Area Home

The Best Way to Start Your Home Search

One of the first steps in your preparation to buy a home should be to start working with a lender to get preapproved for a loan. Without knowing how large a loan you can qualify for, you won't really know the price range where you should be looking. It can be frustrating if you start looking at homes at a certain range and find out later that you will need to settle for a home at a lower price point. Monthly payments are a key part of everyone's budget, so a lender can also help you work backwards from the desired monthly payment to the amount of loan that is affordable. Even experienced homebuyers that have had several mortgagers should still seek the guidance of a lender upfront because lending guidelines change over time and a lender can help match you with a mortgage product that enhances your long-term financial objectives. Getting preapproved in advance provides the confidence for you and a seller that you will be able to close on the loan. In fact, buyers without loan preapproval are at a serious disadvantage when it comes to making an offer on a home. Most sellers will not even consider an offer that is not accompanied with a preapproval letter from a reliable lender. If you find your dream home and are not preapproved, you could lose it to another buyer that was better prepared.

We have several experienced mortgage loan officers to which we can refer buyers and that have competitive rates and have done a good job for our clients. They will take the time to understand your individual needs, help you select a specific mortgage product that is best for you, and will prequalify you for a loan. Although there are national lenders that you can work with online or by telephone, we suggest working with a local lender who is familiar with conditions that vary by locality and can make an impact on a loan.

Along with clarifying your budget, what are you looking for in your new home? We suggest making a list, at least in your mind, of the characteristics that are important. Are you interested in a single-family home or a townhouse or condominium property? What nearby amenities are important for your lifestyle? What size home are you interested in? How far are you willing to commute to work? Do you know which area or areas you desire to live in? Communication of your priorities will help us identify neighborhoods and specific homes that will best meet your needs.

How an Experienced Buyer's Agent Can Help You

Most homes for sale today can be found on the Internet, so some people wonder if they really need a real estate agent to help them purchase a home. Can't they just find houses for sale online and call the listing agents for showings? Of course, that's possible, but who is going to be looking out for your best interests and negotiate on your behalf? If you want a "concierge" type service, an experienced buyer's agent will help you have a seamless and smooth transaction. We will guide you all the way through the process, and it typically doesn't cost a buyer anything, because the commission on the buying side is covered within the listing agent's commission.

As opposed to just responding to a list of homes a buyer wants to see, a buyer's agent will add value throughout the buying process. With knowledge of the market, we can guide buyers to the best places to get the highest resale value. Often, buyers searching the Internet miss homes that might be perfect, but some homes aren't presented well online and they get missed. We can more likely find potential properties that fit their needs. If the buyer wants to avoid certain annoyances, like busy roads or cell towers, we can filter search results, so they're not wasting time opening every potential door.

When the buyer has narrowed down the selection and is getting ready to make an offer, we will analyze the market value and provide insight on a realistic price to offer. Price is a key point of every offer, but other terms are important as well. With knowledge of the buyer's priorities, we can tailor an offer that addresses the buyer's needs while making it attractive to the seller. Having the seller cover certain closing costs is important for some buyers that need to preserve cash, so we will try to work that kind of accommodation into the agreement.

Once a purchase contract is signed, buyers need to complete inspections within the specified time. We have a list of recommended inspectors and contractors that can be used during this phase. When findings arise from an inspection, we will help you interpret the findings and work with you to prepare a response to the seller. Depending on your preferences, we can request the seller to remedy issues prior to closing or you may want to request a credit applied at closing so you can make repairs post-closing. We have vendors, contractors, and other resources that can provide bids on making repairs or changes so you will know the estimated costs before you make a final decision.

Each transaction is unique and working with an experienced buyer's agent can greatly reduce the stress for a buyer as well as delivering the best outcome.

Selecting the Best Agent

A home is usually the most significant financial purchase for an individual or a family. With so much at stake, buyers and sellers should carefully evaluate their options when selecting an agent to represent them. Experience is measured not just in years, but also by the volume of successfully completed transactions. Some real estate websites provide information on agent's past sales. They also provide client reviews which are good indicators of clients' experiences with the agent.

When you interview an agent, try to get a feel for the agent's values, if they align with yours, and if the agent seems to understand your priorities. Do you get a sense the agent will truly represent your best interests in the transaction? Can you trust that the agent can accurately communicate your position to the other side during the negotiations? If you are selling a home, check the marketing materials and methods the agent has used for prior sales and have them specifically talk about what will be done to market your home. Finally, ask for references and check with the references to hear their satisfaction level with the agent.

What Clients Are Saying

"We have worked with Robin several times over the past 10 years and would never consider using anyone else to help us through the buying and selling process. Throughout the process, we deal with Robin directly on all aspects. Awesome is an understatement for the service she provides. I literally texted Robin after 3 years from our last contact and she responded in less than 5 minutes..... which continues throughout our work together. Her sage advice and willingness to listen to our needs, has made our lives simpler during a large transition. She helped us prioritize the fixes, prior to listing our house and our collaborative pricing discussions got our house under contract in less than a month. Robin, helped us through a competitive bid process on our purchase where we came out the winner, while not overpaying for the property."

--RR, Kennesaw, GA

"I can't say enough about Robin. Not only did she make a stressful process run as smoothly as possible but she was always there to listen. Robin knew that we wanted a "forever" home and she didn't stop until we found exactly what we wanted. Thank you so much Robin, we couldn't be happier!"

--AG, Woodstock, GA

"Robin exceeded our home buying and home purchasing expectations. This was a huge transition in our lives and she made it easy and comfortable, handling accurately all the details. Our home sold in a few days and we got more than the asking price! In buying a new home she found exactly what we were looking for!

We can not thank her enough for helping us settle into our new lifestyle and getting us our Dream Home."

--TM, Canton, GA

"Robin Lemon should be everyone's first choice for a realtor. Absolutely the best! After a long period with another realtor we switched to Robin and she was able to sell our home right away. Her guidance throughout the entire process was priceless."

--LM, Roswell, GA

"We loved working with Robin yet again! She is a total professional. From selling our old to getting us into our forever home, we could not be more thrilled with all things Robin. This is the 3rd time we have worked with Robin and we highly recommend her to anyone buying or selling!"

--AA, Woodstock and Roswell, GA

"So thankful for Robin's help with finding our new home! She took the time to get to know us and build a relationship while helping us find our new home. She thoroughly explained the home buying process to us at each step of the journey. While in negotiations, Robin fought hard for us to ensure that we got what was fair. With Robin on our side, we felt the confidence needed to navigate the home buying process."

--VR, Marietta, GA

About Robin Lemon

Robin Lemon has been a licensed real estate agent in Georgia since 2005, when she and her husband moved from Las Vegas. She helps buyers and sellers in the northern suburbs of the Atlanta Metro area and is affiliated with Keller Williams in Roswell, Georgia. Robin has been an award-winning top producer with hundreds of successfully closed real estate transactions. She has continuously been ranked among the top ten individual agents and teams since 2007.

Robin enjoys training and coaching other agents to

succeed on a high level in their own careers. As an Associate Trainer for John Maxwell's Equip Leadership, Inc., she has trained leaders in non-profit organizations and businesses for over 25 years. Robin is involved in the community and has started two non-profit organizations. She has also been a fundraiser and served on several boards. When she resided in Las Vegas, Robin mentored women coming out of the sex industry and is supportive of efforts to end sex trafficking throughout the world.

For more information about Robin Lemon, visit http://www.RobinLemon.net.

The Right Mortgage Is a Critical Part of Successful Real Estate Transactions

Gus Pasquale

Introduction

After graduating from college with a degree in Economics and an interest in real estate finance, Gus Pasquale entered the mortgage industry joining a college football teammate's family-owned mortgage brokerage company in South Florida. Over the past almost 30 years, he has expanded his mortgage practice with ever-increasing business growth.

Gus is a co-founder of Element Funding (2007-present) and is their Division Principal for Element Funding's Florida Operations. Element Funding is focused on mortgage banking for residential home loans in the Southeastern United States. Element Funding helps consumers with financing for home purchases and refinances. Gus and his team also work with builders as a resource for their clients. Element Finding also maintains relationships with real estate agents, financial planners, attorneys, and accountants to coordinate financing for their clients.

In this chapter, Gus Pasquale describes the benefits of working with a local lender that can underwrite and preapprove a mortgage while always closing on time! He stresses the advantages of working with a lender early in the home search process so borrowers can receive counseling on the best mortgage product for their individual needs, financial planning goals, and budget.

Starting to Work with a Lender Early in the Process Generates the Best Results-ALWAYS!

The best time to start working with a mortgage lender is when the notion enters your mind that you want to buy a home, or that you might want to refinance your existing mortgage. Starting the process early helps to validate affordability as well to define the amount that you are eligible for. There are a variety of loan programs and by starting in advance there is time to understand which program best suits your family's needs and financial goals. Frequently I observe people that just shop for a rate and don't stop to consider how to use a mortgage as a financial planning tool.

Going through the process upfront empowers you to

search for homes that are affordable with relative certainty of knowing the payment amount and loan size. It also eliminates wasted time looking at homes that aren't going to be within your budget. Engaging with a mortgage professional early on will strengthen your offer to the seller. The integrity of your offer is validated and solid. Deposit money is not jeopardized, while appraisal fees and inspection fees are not wasted.

By performing the verifications upfront, you know you're getting into the right program, you know the rate and the costs. It's not always just about the amount of loan you can qualify for. Understanding the amount of monthly payment you are comfortable with should be an important factor for people. Sometimes we will work backwards from a budgeted payment and reverse engineer the size of loan and desired down payment. We identify a home price range that will work for you within your budget.

We encourage borrowers to fully participate during the pre-approval phase so we can provide a deep analysis and be as accurate and precise as possible. We proceed all the way to a preapproval with the underwriting upfront if we have all the details of your income and financial situation. This includes review of income breakdown, pay stubs, bank statements, and tax returns as well as pulling a credit report. There's no cost to the consumer to go through this process. It just empowers our team to be able to represent with certainty that you qualify and will be comfortable with the affordability of your home.

We recognize that some clients want to proceed at a pace they are comfortable with because they may just be getting started and are unsure of what they want accomplish. They may provide limited information but not access to the bank statements and tax returns. Perhaps they provide lump sum income, but not how it breaks down including some variable factors. We can provide a prequalification based on the information provided; however such a prequalification may not be completely reflective of actual approval when full underwriting is completed. Entering a purchase contract without preapproval is the most common mistake consumers make when buying a home. Let's say their prequalification was based on income figures they provided, but they did not indicate that the income includes commissions and bonuses. When they get into contract, they provide all the information required for underwriting. But now we find that that not all that income is effective per the regulatory guidelines and it could change the amount of loan they can be qualified for, possibly jeopardizing the ability to close on the home.

It should be an exciting time when purchasing a home, or even when refinancing if you're saving money or making improvements on your home. Underwriting at the front-end builds confidence and reduces the stress of uncertainty as you focus on finding your ideal home. The process is much more comfortable. The mortgage process has the reputation as a frustrating process, yet much of it can be avoided. It could and should be smooth and easy.

The New Era of Mortgage Regulations

Complying with mortgage regulations and guidelines can be frustrating to consumers. They are in place because of the many lesson learned over history. The entire country and the mortgage industry, in particular, learned a lot from the financial crises of 2007. We're lending money, so we must verify the ability to repay, but it's often viewed as much harder than it needs to be. Stricter regulations have been put into place to simultaneously protect the consumer as well as the lender. Specific timeframes have been mandated and the process is now a little less nimble.

The regulations have evolved to insure that the consumer has adequate knowledge of the product being presented and they are comfortable with the affordability of their loan. They are also in place to ensure the consumer receives knowledge of all the costs involved, so that there is no surprise at closing. Timelines have been established so that the consumer has enough time to digest and reflect on the purchase and analyze the cost. The borrower has three days to review the loan estimate and three days to review the closing disclosure. On the lender side, the regulations make sure the loans being made are sustainable and the lenders are not exposed to excessive risk.

These new regulations require a deeper drill down of the consumer and you may feel like you're getting inundated with information requests from us. One lesson that I've learned during my 30 years in the industry is that the loans that move through the process the fastest and come out of underwriting the cleanest are the ones where customers have been very cooperative and timely providing all information requested. They understand that we have the best of intentions to ensure that they qualify. They take our checklists and submit the information as it's outlined. On the other hand, there are people who provide only what they think we need. And that is where it can get a little frustrating for both the borrower as well as the lender.

The Lowest Advertised Rate Is Not Always the Best Solution

It seems like mortgages are being advertised everywhere today, and a common feature of the advertising is the claim of offering the lowest rates. The advertising strives to make consumers believe that mortgages are a commodity and the interest rate is the differentiating factor. The reality is that advertisements are just a marketing tool used to solicit interest of consumers and to try to capture leads. There are only a few levers in mortgage banking and lowest rates historically have had the highest costs. When consumers see a loan that is advertised as the "best rate," it's not always the best fit for them. It's important to do some due diligence to make sure you are comparing relevant factors and understanding the fine print in the offer that discloses that rates are subject to change and to qualification. The best rate loan may be a higher cost loan that exposes the consumer to additional costs and discount points.

Buying and financing a home is one of the largest financial decisions in most people's lives. The market has an overwhelming array of mortgage options for the consumer. For example a 15-year fixed rate mortgage generally has the best fixed rate available. A 15-year loan will put some people in financial hardship because they would struggle to make the required higher payments. The 30-year mortgage has a higher rate, but it has a more affordable payment. The best rate could be an adjustable rate mortgage that keeps the payment low in the short term. However, if staying in the home for several years, borrowers will expose themselves to potential rate increases and payment increases as Federal Reserve and monetary policy changes.

New Technology Is Not a Substitute for Insight, Counseling, and Human Underwriting

The Internet provides a great barometer of ranges of rates but doesn't empower the consumer with insight into tradeoffs and qualifying aspects. Phone apps for mortgages are heavily advertised and have some added value and can ease the application process for the consumer. They are also a great tool for getting consumers to start the process. On the other hand, these apps have created a false sense of security for the consumer because a lot of times they can produce a "false read" in their preapprovals. Based on TV advertising, consumers are led to believe that they can provide minimal information and within a few minutes get preapproved. It's impossible to take a complicated process that historically takes 30 days and accomplish it efficiently and effectively in a few minutes, regardless of the technology.

Online preapprovals are relying on data that's entered by the consumer. The consumer doesn't know the guidelines, so they're just putting in their income. The data that's been entered is run through an automated underwriting system. Let's use commissioned income borrowers as an example. A borrower made $50,000 in a salary position for two years. Recently the consumer entered a sales position with the same company in the third year and went to 100% commission with no track record of consistent commissions. Now that $50,000 is no longer the effective income from an underwriting perspective. So, if the consumer had entered $50,000 as income into the app, an automated underwriting approval would be based on $50,000 per year in income. But later, during the validation phase of the transaction, maybe after a contract was executed, they would find out that the commissioned income isn't effective income. This will affect their qualification. Online mortgage apps cannot replace the personal advisory element that ensures accuracy in the submissions. It may work for some people that are very savvy and understand the mortgage guidelines. It may also work for some people that have very simple circumstances but does not work for most consumers. It's also a big advantage to entertain multiple available options and be counseled rather than just locking into one product.

Sellers and real estate agents on both sides of a real estate transaction also have a stake in making sure that the mortgage financing gets closed on time in a transaction. They are going to push for a local, trusted mortgage expert that has a history of delivering consistently—a local lender that is a phone call or office visit away and one that ALWAYS closes on time.

What You Should and Shouldn't Do After Your Mortgage is Approved

Your preapproval is based on your financial situation at the time of underwriting. It's critical not to do anything that would alter your credit condition before closing on your home. The financial underwriting has already been completed and any changes are subject to a reevaluation. This is not the time to borrow any money, open any new lines of credit, or even apply for additional credit. Some people want to get started looking at furniture for their new home and apply for credit at a furniture store. This can create an alert on a credit inquiry that can jeopardize the mortgage approval.

Don't do anything to alter your employment before you close on your loan. Income stability is a key factor for loan approval. Any change in employment likely will affect the approval status. A better job opportunity may arise but be sure to notify us immediately of any change so we can update any factors that have changed and reevaluate the qualifications.

Be careful with cash deposits into your bank account. Cash deposits that cannot be paper-trailed to specific effective sources of funds are not eligible to be used for the transaction. This includes use for a down payment or for an earnest money deposit. Additionally, large cash deposits raise a red flag in an age where financial institutions are involved in monitoring for Homeland Security Reporting and money laundering concerns.

You will have submitted many documents to your lender starting at the preapproval stage. I suggest keeping a file folder with all the documents related to your mortgage and home purchase in one file for easy access throughout the process. This file should include everything that you have submitted to the lender and everything related to your interaction with the Title Company and real estate agent. Sometimes people take pictures of documents with their phone and submit images that aren't completely legible. In this case you may be asked to resubmit one or more documents.

Keep all current pay stubs. Sometimes the sellers are not ready to close on the original date and the closing may be moved out. Your lender will be asking for the most recent pay stub before closing. Keep all your current pay stubs in your document folder.

Selecting a Mortgage Professional

The expertise and trust of a mortgage professional on the front end really hasn't been more important than it is today because consumers are in overwhelm mode when it comes to the information. Your computer screen starts to look like the glitz and glamour of Manhattan when you start looking for homes or mortgages online and the mortgage companies target you with offers. The Internet is a great research tool and barometer of rates and programs, but what's missing is the insight to make sense of it all and find the best program for you and your family. Do not deprive yourself of that expertise.

The best approach is to work with a trusted, tenured lending organization that provides the expertise and processing efficiency to accurately qualify you as well counsel on the best product for your circumstances and financial goals. The Internet will never replace that. A local lender allows a personal touch as well as familiarity with local market conditions. Element Funding's preapproval process has given real estate agents a sense of security to the tens of thousands of local homeowners we serve. They recognize the effective operational expertise we operate within and that we will get each loan to the finish line on time, ALWAYS!

A significant amount of our volume is what we define as rescue loans where the borrower has gone to a national call center or to an Internet portal lender. Then at the 11th hour, that lender couldn't close on time and the buyer is 16 days into a 30-day closing and they are being asked by the lender to get an extension for another two weeks. Real estate agents don't want to hear that and don't want to extend the closing. Assuming the borrower has all their information compiled and in order, we can take their submission, put it into our system and have our underwriter rapidly complete the approval and be able to close in 15 days. Our ability to be nimble as a local team is a big aid to help agents rescue and complete deals that might have otherwise fallen apart.

Consumers can enter our process and submit applications through several options: on a phone call, online, through our phone app, or the old school way, in person at one of our offices. Regardless how they enter our process, we provide counseling to help them select the best program and we thoroughly review the submissions for accuracy.

At Element Funding, we tell people that we put the fun in funding. We really tried to make obtaining a mortgage a better process and value proposition. We coach the consumer to get us everything on the checklist to help us make each mortgage transaction easy and successful.

What Element Funding Associates Are Saying

"Over the last 8 years I have had the privilege of working alongside Gus and the Element brand. I have been in the business for 24 years and I can hands down say Gus has made me feel at home, welcomed me and my family, along with embracing each milestone with my team and I. Gus is not only involved, but genuinely cares about each of us; and to me, that makes all the difference in the world."

--DeAnn Ellis, Senior Loan Officer,
NMLS: 148916

"Having worked alongside Gus at Element Funding since the very beginning I have watched him grow Element into an incredible company that cares about each employee and client we serve with the highest level of service. Element Funding at its core is based on treating each other as family and with respect for one another. These values I believe reflects in how we as associates represent Element Funding day in and day out in the communities we serve with our realtors, builders and clients. There is truly no better company to work for."

--Nichole Manor, Branch Manager/Mortgage Banker,
NMLS: 399002

"In the 25 years working in the mortgage space I've worked for 3 companies. Why, because it's all about the people you work with who make the difference. Buying/financing a home is considered one of the most stressful events in a person's lifetime. We at

Element Funding all have the same common principles, do what's right for the customer while working cohesively internally so the customer feels no stress. Also, the management team recognizes us as family and not as just an employee and they truly listen and care. They live to serve, internally and externally. I would not be here for close to 10 years if were any other way. Great people = great company."

--Maurice Kalter, Loan Originator,
NMLS: 277961

"One of the more challenging aspects of the home buying experience is the mortgage process. At Element Funding, our platform is designed with the customer in mind and runs like a well-oiled machine. Our Operations Team is in totally alignment with the front end, loan officers, when it comes to making sure that the mortgage process is NOT the most challenging. Everyone on my team, from loan set up, to processing, to underwriting, to closing and even post-closing, totally understand the mission of delivering complete customer satisfaction! We want to create raving fans, who tell their friends, family and coworkers that the horror stories that surround our industry must be folklore because it just doesn't happen here. The surveys come back and validate we are doing it right!!!"

--Lane Baton, Mortgage Laon Originator,
NMLS: 332466

"I joined the Element Funding team in February 2009. While looking for employment, I thought about the company and asked myself if it was the place for me. Every company develops a

corporate persona that may or may not fit someone's personality. This persona encompasses many things from ethics to goals to the type of people hired. Element Funding is the right fit for me. The positive atmosphere at Element Funding is noticeable at all levels. People are helpful and caring. There's a 'can do' attitude that starts from management and winds its way into every department.

"Our goal is to serve not just our borrowers, but the realtors, the title companies and every other Element Funding employee as well. People feel appreciated and are recognized for their dedication and hard work. There is certainly a rare energy from the top down that is contagious. Employees are encouraged to acknowledge co-workers for their hard work and accomplishments. All levels of management are approachable. When an issue arises, there is always someone that will try and help come up with a solution. We are truly a team... a family. I know this is the right place for me."

--Carly Schulman, Branch Support Specialist

About Gus Pasquale

Gus Pasquale has almost 30 years in the mortgage industry and his career started when fixed rate mortgages were in the high teens and adjustable rates in the low teens. He has had a front row seat to market cycles from the boom, the bust, and the recovery. His expertise has been in residential and builder mortgages with personal productivity eclipsing $900 million in production.

Gus was a co-founder of Element Funding and his team has approached the $3 billion threshold in on time closings since Element Funding was founded.

Element Funding was launched in 2007 at the worst time in the history of mortgage banking and has guided almost 30,000 families into secure home loans in the Southeastern United States.

Originally from Yonkers, New York, Gus has been a South Florida resident for 38 years. He is a graduate of Cornell College (Iowa) with a Bachelor of Science Degree in Economics, where he was four-year letterman in football. Gus has been recognized as The Gold Coast Builder's Association "Lender of the Year," "Top Gun Originator," and "Presidents Award/Achiever" in each of his years in the production channel. His personal and professional mantra is LIVE2SERVE.

For more information abut Gus Pasquale and Element Funding, visit http://www.ElementFuniding.com.

NMLS: 334373

Sell for More Money, Faster, with Less Stress. Here's How

Christine Rich

Introduction

After a successful career as a marketing consultant, Christine Rich decided to apply her marketing acumen and problem-solving skills in the world of real estate. Having bought and sold multiple homes across the DC area before becoming an agent, she saw first-hand that she could provide a better and more client-focused experience for people. Her goal is always to create a hugely successful outcome for her clients.

Today, Christine is an award-winning real estate agent helping people across the metro DC area to successfully sell and buy homes, consistently ranking among the top agents in the region. She is licensed in DC, Virginia, and Maryland.

In this chapter Christine provides insights for homeowners in the Washington, D.C. metro area—specifically Northern Virginia—who are interested in selling their homes for the highest price possible, quickly, and with minimum stress.

Getting Prepared to Sell Your Home

Every homeowner is unique, and each has different objectives when it comes to selling their home. As an agent, it's critical that I understand my clients' motivations to be able to provide the highest level of service in meeting their needs. Getting the most out of the home sale is important to everyone, but what about the timing of the sale? Is there a desire or need to be out of the home at a specific time? We need discuss the market situation and time of year and how those factors will affect the time to sell. Many people are interested in buying a new home and selling simultaneously. Given our client's financial situation we will work out the best strategy to accomplish this. I'll also review the condition of the property and advise on cost-effective updates, if appropriate, that will yield the best outcome—a quick sale at a price above asking price with minimal contract contingencies.

Buyers are very savvy today, so we want to be able to anticipate how they will be evaluating the home and questions they are likely to be asking. They will have some perspective on values from sites that provide value estimates and they will be able to see other recent home sale prices in the area on some of these sites. Homeowners know their own property the best, so I always want to get their perspective on their property. What are the ages of the roof, appliances, and major systems? What updates and renovations have been done and when? What have they enjoyed the most about their home? What are the best features of the neighborhood? This information will help tell the story of the home when we are putting together our marketing program and materials.

It's important to have a clear understanding on how involved the homeowner wants to be in the process. In my experience some clients want to be very hands-on, while others prefer to hand-off virtually everything to me, even the schedule and direction on when they need to be prepared to move out. Communications expectations during the process should also be discussed. What communication methods and frequency do the sellers prefer? Best results usually follow when the sellers and agent are on the same page with respect to expectations.

Pricing for the Best Outcome

I mentioned earlier about the online price estimates that most buyers are going to see. It's important to know that these estimates are not necessarily correct, and they are mostly based on statistics and not some of the critical indicators of value, such as location, condition, and level of upgrades and renovations. I use a very thorough approach to estimating market value and it's consistent with the way an appraiser analyzes the value. I look at several comparable properties that have sold nearby in the past six months and then adjust to reflect differences between the comparable sales and your property. I also factor in market conditions. Are we in a rising or falling market? I also factor in what I call the "art" of selling the home. Are there features or elements of the home that we can communicate that will energize buyers and create a bidding war? Once I've established the best estimate, I may also test the pricing with other agents in the market to get their reaction.

A homeowner can sometimes net a larger profit on sale by making some updates prior to listing the home. When I observe this opportunity, I will analyze two scenarios. The first is for a sale of the home as-is. The second is for the home after appropriate updates have been completed. In the second case, I'll provides estimates for the cost of changes and a value based on the updates being completed prior to going on the market. I've found that the return on investment can be substantial depending on the condition of the home and the homeowner's ability to invest in the improvements.

Listing the property at the correct market price is critical to attracting buyers to schedule a showing. If we price too high, even by a small amount, the property will sit on the market and our Days on Market will just increase without much action. The local market has been strong for several years and after about two weeks without a contract, buyers and their agent will suspect something is wrong with the property. It's all downhill from there as you will need to reduce the price, maybe more than once, and doubt among buyers and agents just increases. It's okay if we happen to err on the side of being slightly low. The low inventory and strong demand this market has experienced over many years will attract many buyers in this case, and will create a bidding war, driving up the ultimate price.

What about Selling to a Builder?

The Washington, D.C. area market has experienced rapid increases in value over recent years to the point where lot prices for new construction in desirable areas are very expensive. With a shortage of lots available for new construction, builders are frequently buying older houses, tearing them down, and building new expensive homes on the properties. The value of a lot can exceed $1 million in certain areas. Homeowners frequently receive solicitations from builders promising to buy their home for market value for cash and no hassle, but builders will only offer a low price for the lot, unless they are in competition with others.

If the home has been neglected, has mold or water damage, or is in complete disrepair, selling to a builder could be a viable option. It also might be an option if the home has functional obsolescence and the cost to make improvements is so high that the homeowner can net as much or as close to the same net amount without all the work. It's important to keep in mind that it is not a given that your property will be attractive to a builder. The specific location, size and shape of the lot, and the terrain all are critical for a builder. If selling to a builder is an option you want to explore, I can provide an evaluation of the potential for sale to a builder and the market value of your property as-is. If this is a good option, I can create a marketing campaign to attract builders and create a bidding war for the property. This is more likely to generate a higher price than just selling directly to a builder who sent you a postcard. There are also buyers who are interested in building their own home on a nice lot, or in buying a starter home that they can renovate, and our marketing efforts will be directed to them as well.

Preparing Your Home for Sale to the General Public

How you sell your property for the most money possible is very different from how you live in your home. When selling your home, we are marketing a product. Some relatively small adjustments will yield big results.

Styles and trends change over time and buyers rarely have the vision to see beyond what is presented to them. Bright colors on the walls may have been in style a couple of decades ago, but today buyers prefer neutral colors. TV home improvement shows invariably feature a "before view" of a home with bright red or other strong colors on walls with a lot of negative comments. You don't want to be that home with the red walls. A fresh coat of paint works miracles, and the popular trend today is a light neutral grey-beige tone. Light colored walls even make the home seem brighter and larger.

Pay particular attention to the front of the home where buyers will be parking and walking up to the front door. The landscaping should be well maintained, the grass trimmed, and planting beds cleared of weeds and fresh mulch applied. Depending on the time of year, flowers will add some color. The front door and porch should be clean and free of cobwebs. Buyers will be paying attention as they walk up to your front door, anticipating what they will be seeing inside. The front door may benefit from a fresh coat of paint—today there's a popular blue color that's very inviting to visitors. The windows should be cleaned so they will let light into the home and not have evidence of dirt or webs when looking outside from the interior.

A home must first and foremost be clutter-free and clean to create an emotionally compelling presentation. This often means removing about half of the owners' personal items from the home. Countertops should be cleared of everything but the bare necessities. Tops of dressers need to be cleared and books and other items should be removed from shelving so at least half of the space is empty. Some people have a lot of artwork and personal items on the walls and many of these items should be removed as well. We want buyers to focus on the home itself, not all the owner's possessions. Early in the process I'll walk with you through your home and provide suggestions on de-cluttering. I often bring in a staging consultant to advise on the best arrangement of furniture and artwork. We'll frequently recommend removing some of the furniture to open up pathways and reduce crowding. The objective is to make the home appear as spacious and open as possible so buyers can envision their furniture and possessions fitting in the home.

If the homeowners have already moved from the house, staging the home will help it sell for the highest price. A vacant home doesn't present well, whether viewing photos of empty rooms online or when walking through the home and it's a challenge for people to imagine their furniture in an empty home.

After the home is prepared and de-cluttered, we will bring in a professional photographer to take pictures that will show off the home at its best. Most buyers start looking at homes online and decide whether to tour the home based on the photos they see. Our goal is to present the home with photos that are appealing and enticing, so buyers are motivated to request a showing. Our photographer will consider the lighting based on time of day and will capture the photos in the most attractive lighting. Our photographer often uses fusion photography which takes more time in the processing, but the final images are really beautiful. We want to make sure all the important features are captured, and rooms are shown from the best angles to make our listings stand out.

Along with pricing that reflects market value, presentation is critical to attracting potential buyers and achieving the best outcome. In my previous life as a marketing professional, we always crafted our marketing campaigns to both persuade through reason and motivate through emotion, meaning the property should be priced right and look attractive. Buyers may say that they can see beyond paint colors and clutter, but they are much more likely to emotionally connect with a home that has been professionally prepared and presented.

Marketing That Works to Sell Your Home

As mentioned earlier, our local market has experienced several years of low inventories coupled with high demand. Because of this situation many homeowners think that it's easy to sell a home in this area and all homes will sell quickly. That's really not true. Presentation and pricing are critical and so is exposure to the most relevant potential buyers. Marketing makes a big difference between homes that sell quickly for more money, and those that linger on the market, ultimately with price reductions along the way, and netting a lower price in the end.

The best marketing strategy starts with a vision of who the buyer is for your home. With an understanding of the buyer profile that the home will function for or appeal to the most, we can tailor the marketing approach to target and reach these buyers. As an example, a suburban home in a great school district may appeal to young families with children living in the city. They may desire more space to grow their family and want to live in an excellent school district, but still have an easy commute into the city. A smaller home with the bedrooms on the ground floor may appeal to a couple looking to downsize.

We can target buyers based on their likely profile and reach them beyond the standard Multiple Listing Service (MLS) feed. In this way we can promote the property in a well-orchestrated marketing program that focuses on channels where our prospective buyers are spending time and paying attention and maximize market exposure while creating excitement in the marketplace. There are websites that appeal to families who are moving out from DC to the Virginia suburbs and others that appeal to people currently living further away but want to move to a closer suburban area.

Another valuable tool is a professional brochure that we leave in the home for buyers to review during showings and take away so they can remember the home. The description in the brochure is written with an emotional appeal and speaks directly to our target buyers. This is another place we use several of the photos so the people can see and remember the most important features of the home. I've had buyers tell me at the closing that from the day they took our brochure, through the agreement stage, all the way up to closing, they have enjoyed looking at the brochure, imagining themselves living in the home. It's another way to solidify an emotional connection to the home.

Showings

Showing your home is an inconvenient but a necessary aspect of selling your home. There's a much better opportunity to sell your home quickly if you provide the most flexibility in making the home available for showings. We can request notice from as little as 1 hour up to 24 hours in advance, but remember many buyers are on a schedule and may have limited time to view homes, especially if they are moving into the area. If they can't conveniently see your home, they probably will be touring others, and they may make an offer on another property because they couldn't see yours on their schedule.

It may be tiresome to keep your home show-ready, but the home needs to stay clean during this time. Beds should be made, dirty dishes not left in the sink, and everything nicely organized throughout the house. Homeowners should be away from the home during showings because buyers don't feel comfortable looking through a home when the owners are present. Pets, especially dogs and cats, should not be present in the home during showings.

Negotiating the Contract

An offer is the starting point for negotiating a purchase contract for your home. Price is always important, but timing and contingencies are also key points. Buyers and sellers generally want diametrically opposite results. Seller would like a cash purchase with a high price without contingencies. Buyers are interested in the lowest possible price with as many contingencies they can get to best protect themselves through the transaction. It comes down to negotiating the best contract so that both sides feel that they have won. We may have one offer, or we may have multiple offers for your home. In either case, I will carefully review the offer or offers and advise on the pros and cons of each.

Most buyers require mortgage financing and we always expect to have a pre-approval letter from the lender submitted with the offer. I always speak with the lender to understand, beyond just the letter how qualified the buyers are. If the buyer is using a lender not familiar to me, I will make inquiries of lenders I know to try to get as much information as possible to make sure it's a reliable company as well as a responsive loan officer. The last thing we want is to enter into a contract with a buyer and find out much later in the process that the buyer is not able to get the funding approved.

The reputation of the buyer's agent can be a relevant factor on how smoothly a transaction will proceed. While most agents act in a professional manner, some agents have a reputation of causing problems during the transaction. This can be a red flag and caution is advised, knowing in advance that such an agent is difficult to work with.

Most of the time the offers don't address all the seller's needs, so I'll work to negotiate the offers toward the best position for the seller. This may take a few iterations and I've been known to spend many hours in the evening working the offers so that in the end the sellers have netted thousands more from these negotiations.

Contract to Closing

The contract is signed but there still may be some obstacles to overcome before we can get to the closing. Schedules and contingencies must be monitored, and often one or more problems arise that need a quick solution. It takes diligence during this time to ensure we are quickly developing solutions to issues that arise. After all, we want smiles all around at the settlement.

Most contracts provide for the buyers to have one or more inspections done on the home. A general home inspection is typical, but there may also be a radon test or other specialized inspections depending on the type and location of property. The buyer's inspection may note some items that need to be repaired, so this can start some additional negotiations to reach agreement on addressing issues in the inspection report. Depending on the findings, we will quickly gather estimates to complete the repairs and work on behalf of the seller to reach agreement. One option is to have the seller complete the work prior to closing. Another option is to negotiate a credit to the buyers in lieu of the seller doing the work. At the end of the day the seller wants to sell, and the buyer wants to buy, so we want to reach agreement that makes sense for both.

There will usually be an appraisal contingency if the buyer will be using mortgage financing to purchase the home. In the most common case, the contingency calls for the appraisal to come in at or above the negotiated sales price. Since we've done our homework on market value in advance of the listing and priced the home correctly, we usually don't have an issue with the appraisal. The most frequent issue with the appraisal is when we have a lot of competition among buyers for a home and the price gets bid up beyond the listing price. When there's a lot of competition, buyers may also offer an escalation clause, offering to beat any other offer by a certain amount. When either of these conditions occur, we try to negotiate away from an appraisal contingency in the purchase contract to minimize risk for the seller.

The other typical contingency is for the final approval of the buyer's mortgage financing. Nothing is ever completely certain, but our vetting of the buyer and lender during the contract negotiation removes most of the risk in this area.

Selecting an Agent to Sell Your Home

A home is a very valuable financial asset, the largest asset for most families and individuals. If you are going to sell a valuable asset, I'd advise seeking an expert who will help you achieve the highest possible price and make your transaction as smooth as possible. A sales record with a high volume of successfully completed real estate transactions is one indicator. Online reviews and testimonials are another indicator of how clients have benefited from working with an agent.

An important statistic is the ratio of sales price to list price. A high ratio is an indicator of market knowledge, proper pricing, and successful marketing. Inquire how the agent will be marketing your home. Look at the photos in the agent's online listings. Do they present the listing in a professional manner that makes the home stand out? Ask to see other marketing materials the agent typically uses. Do they reflect a professional approach? It costs money to properly market a home and reviewing how the agent has marketed other homes provides an indicator that the agent has a budget to market your home.

Selling your home can be an intense process and significant money is at stake. Make sure you and your agent are aligned on expectations for the result as well as the communications preferences through the process. I would also make sure that there is a good match in terms of personality and that you have a good feeling that the agent is someone you can trust and who will be looking out for your best interests at all times.

What Clients Are Saying

"We contacted Christine more than a year before we were intending to list our home. She was very accommodating in meeting with us periodically as we prepared to move out of the area. She was very informative and provided excellent recommendations to us as we readied our home for sale. When the time came to list, her additional support and professional approach was tremendous! We greatly appreciated working with her and have highly recommend her to our friends."

"Christine exceeded expectations with both the sale and purchase of homes nearly concurrently. She had a contract on the selling home within one day on the market and through expert advice, strong negotiating skills, and keen insight led to a quick contract for the new home purchase. She worked flawlessly and seamlessly through all the different and technical aspects of both transactions that kept everything on track and on-time! Highly detailed oriented, extremely professional and courteous! Highly recommended and would use again for any future transactions!"

"We had initially had our house listed with another agent and were not happy with the offers we had gotten. She took on the listing in the late Summer. Immediately she helped us with staging and updating the look of the house. Her suggestions were not costly but had a huge impact (e.g, she suggested painting the shutters which made the house look great). We got more traffic and a couple of low offers. Chris actively negotiated with the buyers' agents to the point where we finally got an offer that reflected the value of the property and sold the house. We would strongly recommend Chris for anyone looking for a great realtor!"

"Christine Rich gave us outstanding help when we bought a new home and sold our old one. Last Fall we decided to move. I found on Zillow that Christine was the selling agent for a house in our neighborhood that was hard to sell, and it sold for more than expected. We contacted her and she met with us that week. Christine was friendly, listened to our wishes, and had great ideas for us. She helped us find exactly the new home we wanted in just a day. Then she helped us negotiate a good price. Christine next quickly got us a great offer and contract on our own hard-to-sell house. And she knew other people who could help with the details of downsizing and relocating. We highly recommend working with Christine."

"Christine is a real pro and a real pleasure to work with. We followed her advice on preparing the house (even when we didn't want to), she set up excellent marketing locally and online, and mostly we talked and talked about the market -- comparables, sensitivities, market activity, how to get the best price we could in the time-frame we needed. And then? A full-price offer in four hours. We couldn't be more grateful."

"Christine helped so much with our move. We were being relocated with the government to the other side of the country. We left and were so comfortable leaving our home and it's sale in her hands. She took care of so much, from arranging staging, minor repairs, painting touch-ups, and cleaning. We were so pleased with how our home was marketed. She definitely respected our wishes about that. However I am most grateful for how she handled things once we had a contract. Being so far away, we so respect that she took care of many things for us. We had a challenging period where the buyers had firm expectations about what needed to happen

for them to purchase the house. She got multiple folks to evaluate and make binding estimates for us. This all worked out in the end but only because of her diligence and perseverance. Our house sold in less than sixty days. I cannot say enough positive things about all she did to help us. We are very grateful! And we highly and without reservation recommend her!"

About Christine Rich

Christine Rich is an award-winning real estate agent in the Washington, D.C. area, currently affiliated with Long and Foster in the Arlington, Virginia office. She helps buyers and sellers with their real estate transactions in the Washington, D.C. metro area. Before entering the real estate field, Christine was a successful communications and marketing vice president at a local political consulting firm where she advised corporate and non-profit clients on how to best market and communicate about their organizations.

Christine became interested in real estate after realizing that she could improve the real estate experience for clients by providing honest, straightforward advice and guidance while focusing on her clients' needs and desires. She gained rapid success in the industry and today ranks as the #15 agent across all of the state of Virginia.

Christine's recent awards for real estate sales excellence include:

- Arlington Magazine Top Producer 2019

- #1 Agent Arlington Office, Long and Foster

- Washingtonian Best Agent – Platinum Level – 2015-2019

- Northern Virginia Magazine Top Agent

- Top 100 Agents DC, Metro Real Producers

- Real Trends Inc. Top 1000 Agents

- Zillow 5-Star Agent

For more information about Christine Rich, visit https://www.ChristineRich.com.

Kick Off Your Home Search with the Right Lender

Frank Bennett

Introduction

Frank Bennett had a brief career selling real estate for a homebuilder. He didn't have a great experience with the lending institutions the homebuilder required their agents to use because too many customer loans were getting rejected. A loan officer at one of the lenders suggested that he might be better off working the lending side of the transactions. Frank was hired as a loan officer and his first objective was working with prior customers whose loans had been rejected. After studying the guidelines, he was able to rapidly get six of the customers qualified that had previously been turned down by other loan officers.

After over 30 years in the mortgage industry Frank and his team help people with their residential purchase financing and refinancing in the entire state of Georgia and in the Florida Panhandle area. He works with clients from first time homebuyer to luxury home purchasers, as well as with credit challenged people.

In this chapter, Frank stresses the importance of starting to work with a lender before looking for a home, why a local lender is better than a national online lender for most borrowers, and best practices for handling finances after getting preapproved for a mortgage and before closing.

Preapproval Should Be the First Step in Searching for a New Home

Getting a mortgage preapproval is the best way to start your search for a new home. You don't want to waste a lot of time shopping for a home until you are sure of what price range home you can afford. During the preapproval process we will request information and documentation about your income, expenses, and assets so we can verify the information. We will also obtain a credit report and run your information through our automated underwriting system. The outcome will indicate the maximum loan that you will qualify for as well as the monthly payments. Even if qualified for a loan at a certain level, most people are interested in an affordable monthly payment, so we can also reverse engineer a borrower's budgeted monthly payment and their anticipated down payment into a price range for a property that will work.

Going through this exercise frequently results in finding out that you can qualify for a larger loan than you had anticipated. Instead of having to settle for a smaller home, you may find that you can purchase a larger home that may be more suitable for your family.

Preapproval is now almost a prerequisite for looking at homes from the perspective of real estate agents. Experienced agents generally don't want to waste time showing homes until they see a preapproval letter from a reliable lender. Additionally, seller's agents won't recommend to their seller considering offers without a preapproval letter. If you wait to apply for a mortgage until you find the home you want buy, you stand a good chance of losing the opportunity to another buyer that is already prepared. Real estate agents like to have a high level of confidence in the loan officer and company that has issued the preapproval. It's pretty common now for agents to go beyond the preapproval letter and they want to talk directly to the loan officer to make sure all relevant information has been personally verified and they get a comfortable indication that the loan is going to get funded. We won't disclose confidential financial data to the agent, but we can give a highly confident answer on the ability of the loan to close.

Borrowers with excellent credit, a simple financial profile with long-term income stability, and solid down payment money saved up are usually very easy to get qualified; however, there are many factors that can affect the ability to qualify. Self-employment income is a little bit more unique. We are going to be looking at the income in the last two full years and current year-to-date and then average the income. Since the income fluctuates, we'll take an average rather than just looking at the last month's income. People that have variable income from commissions or bonuses are similar. Moving cash around right before buying a home is a red flag and it's better to understand the ramifications in advance, before you start looking for a home.

Another outcome of a consultation with a loan officer is getting educated on the variety of loan programs that might be available and to help you select a mortgage product that best matches your mid to long-term financial objectives. Some people avoid thinking about buying a home because they may not have saved up enough money for a down payment. There are loan programs available for first-time homebuyers and some of the loan products we offer require only a very small or even no down payment.

When a borrower is not presently qualified for a loan or not a large enough loan, I'll work with them to outline the recommended steps they can take so they can get qualified. This is not the same as credit repair; but with knowledge of the levers involved in credit worthiness and the regulatory guidelines for a variety of mortgage options, I can suggest how to transform a borrower's financial situation so they can qualify. In some cases, it could just take a couple of months to improve their case, while it might take a year or so for other people. I really enjoy this part of my work, because so many times I have been able to help individuals and families achieve their dream of home ownership.

It's Not Just About the Rate

For some people, it's tempting to look at the advertised rates and seek out the lender who is advertising the lowest interest rate loan. The interest rate is important, but for most people the actual monthly payment is the most important factor. An advertised low rate may be for a shorter-term loan that will have a higher payment than a more typical 30-year loan. In addition to the interest rate there may be fees (or points) involved in the transaction that get capitalized into the loan and also private mortgage insurance if the down payment is less than 20%. Don't forget about escrow for taxes and insurance that are usually included in the monthly payment. Borrowers need to do their research when making comparisons to make sure they are comparing similar loan programs.

Our company focuses on helping borrowers get the best payment option possible. If that includes the best rate, it's great. We have programs that provide for lender paid mortgage insurance or split payment insurance, so there are different options to lower the payment. It's not unusual to see someone quoting a lower interest rate but when comparing payments, ours is less.

Peace of mind should be another consideration. If you are shopping based on interest rate, are you comparing the reputation of the lenders and loan officers to be able to deliver on time and provide excellent service? Today's purchase contracts usually have several contingencies which require a strict compliance with timing as specified in the contract. As a borrower, you are depositing earnest money that can be a substantial sum. An appraisal contingency may be for 10 to 14 days. If the lender is not efficient and misses the deadline for the appraisal, and the appraisal comes back low, you could lose your earnest money deposit. There's typically a 21-day period for approval of the financing. If the lender can't get it done within the proscribed period, you have another opportunity to lose your deposit and the seller can sell their home to another buyer. How does it feel now if the lender you chose because of a quoted rate difference of say one eight percent less causes you to lose the opportunity to buy the new home and you lose your deposit at the same time? On a $200,000 loan, the rate difference may be less than $20.00 per month.

Best Practices After Preapproval Up to the Closing

Mortgage preapproval is based on the financial information submitted and changes to a borrower's financial profile before closing on a home can jeopardize the preapproval. I provide a checklist of do's and don'ts when purchasing a home—another reason for communicating with a lender early in your home search endeavor.

The most obvious thing is not taking on any more debt after preapproval. Maintain your current bank accounts, don't open new bank accounts, and don't excessively run up balances on your credit cards. This is not the time to buy a new auto, apply for additional credit lines, purchase furniture with financing for your new home, or making any other new debt commitments. This also applies for co-signing a loan, say on a relative's auto. When your credit is run again for final approval any new debt will be discovered and may invalidate your preapproval.

Something that comes up a lot is the borrower gets an opportunity to change jobs and get an increase in pay. It's not always a deal killer as long as it's in the same line of work and demonstrates upward mobility. For the most part we caution if you are thinking about changing jobs you might want to do it immediately and then wait until you've at least got a month's worth of pay stubs and after we can show that you are no longer on probation. Another alternative is to try to wait until after closing on your new home which will make it less of hassle for you. Unpaid leave from work is another thing to avoid. This will affect year-to-date income and will be an issue when your loan is being finalized.

Not so obvious, but one if the largest problems during this period is cash deposits into your bank accounts. The source of funds for your down payment needs to be traced to approved sources and should already be in your bank account before you apply for financing. Cash deposits raise suspicions about the source of funds, so they need to be avoided. You may have some cash laying around or be given cash as a gift, but don't deposit before closing. The only money flowing into your bank account should be your normal paycheck deposits. Let's say you decide to sell a vehicle and want to deposit the proceeds. In order to properly trace, we need to get the bill of sale for the car, the transfer of title, and a Kelly Blue Book or NADA value on the car. There are a lot more hoops to jump through to trace the source of cash.

The Truth About Online Lenders and the Few Minute Preapproval Process

I talked earlier about the importance of starting to work with a lender at the beginning of your home search process. If you watch or listen to advertising from some of the national online mortgage companies, you probably will get a different impression. Advertisements show homebuyers getting ready to make an offer on a home and using an app to get approved in less than ten minutes. The reality is that these apps rely on data entered by the borrower and there is not any verification of the financial data to substantiate income or assets at this stage. Over time, real estate agents became leery of such preapprovals because so many deals have blown up because the loans couldn't get closed. Many times, when a buyer shows a preapproval from an online lender the agent requires the client to also get a preapproval from a local lender known to be reliable. In the end, the borrower may decide to get the mortgage through the online lender, but at least the agents and seller can get confidence with a local preapproval.

Online lenders can be a viable option for some people that have an excellent financial profile with a 20% down payment that has been sitting in a bank account for several months, a stable employment history on their job for many years, a great credit score, and have no situations with bankruptcies, divorces, leases on properties, co-signed notes where the other person on the loan didn't make a payment on time, or deferred student loans. The online lenders are generally not good at dealing with curve balls or when you need a letter of explanation of the borrower's situation. They are most interested in pushing a volume of loans and don't have the resources or desire to work through more challenging borrower situations. Another characteristic is that you are probably going to be talking to a different person every time you call, so there's not likely to be consistency or accountability to make sure your loan closes on time.

Our approach is quite a bit different. Instead of trying to fit our clients into a specific loan package we offer a variety of programs. We also enjoy the challenge of helping borrowers who have been turned down at other lenders. Even if we can't prequalify you, we will advise on what you need to do to get yourself into a position so you can qualify. Sometimes it's creativity in asking the right questions and finding a solution that will work.

I have a short story about a borrower we helped with a complex situation even when other lenders were not able to help. Someone I know asked me to meet with a couple from South America that wanted to buy a house. They didn't speak English, but my friend was bilingual. I verified their income and other information and did a credit check. When asked about the source of a down payment, they said they planned to sell an apartment property they owned in South America. That was going to be difficult to document. Since the borrowers were interested in an FHA loan, I asked if they had a relative they could borrow the down payment from, since that is allowed with an FHA loan. They did have a relative that could make a short-term loan. The only other obstacle was the borrower had only been working in the United States for one year and nine months and the guidelines require a full two years of continuous employment, so they were going to have to wait three months. It takes a little out-of-the-box thinking, but there are solutions available to help people qualify for a mortgage. This type of case is where the typical online lender would just say you don't qualify and not offer ideas or alternatives that will put you into a position to qualify.

What Clients Are Saying

"Lets just say that when you are wanting to refinance your home, there are a lot of sharks out in the water waiting for you to make a move. Well, I have never refinanced a home before and was bombarded by phone calls and letters in the mail from different lenders wanting me to go with them. So let me go ahead and say that I went with Frank and his team. He answered all my questions right off the bat! Won me over right then and there. Frank and his whole team worked fast and got my loan done in no time at all. No pressure and stress free! Thank you and appreciate all the hard work involved!!"

--Christy H.

"We highly recommend Frank and his team. The team was completely committed to making our dreams come true. My husband and I previously had a terrible experience with another big loan company only a few months before. The previous company had brushed us off so quickly. Our situation was unique and would require more work. From day one Frank reassured us that they would do everything in their power to get us in our dream home. There were late night calls, numerous emails and consistency. Frank, Melanie and Kim never gave up on us."

--Nayara T.

"Frank & his team are amazing! They are so kind & patient and are always willing to answer any questions and/or concerns you may have. My husband & I truly enjoyed working with them. Great customer service!"

--Bud and Kassie M.

"Frank really knows the market and the marketplace of products and helped me to tailor my loan to meet our needs. I can't thank him enough! I definitely recommend him."

--John K.

"I cannot say enough about What Frank and his team did for me on my first home buyer experience. I had no idea where to start or what buying a home even entailed. Frank met with me and laid out everything I needed to do to get the house I wanted. This wasn't easy as the complex I was buying in wasn't FHA approved but Frank took it upon himself to help get my complex approved! Don't know many lenders who would do that. They communicated with me every step of the way and worked endlessly to meet my closing deadline. I cannot thank Frank and his team enough for all they did for me. I would recommend them to anyone and I will use them again when I am ready to buy."

--Paige N.

"Recently I returned to the home buying market after retiring and relocating to Georgia. I needed a loan officer who was equipped with an engaging staff and support system that could navigate me through the maze of needed documents and the patience of Job. Element, Frank and his staff delivered beyond expectations and today I reside in a wonderful home in Georgia. It is my opinion and first hand knowledge that if you have the opportunity to work with Element, Frank and his staff you will not regret your decision."

--Hersey

About Frank Bennett

Frank Bennett has been helping people with their residential financing needs since 1986. He has served as Sales Manager, Branch Manager, and Regional Production Manager. Frank is affiliated with Element Funding and serves as a Loan Officer and Branch Manager in Alpharetta, Georgia and in Miramar Beach, Florida. He works with clients throughout the state of Georgia and in the Florida Panhandle area. Frank's area of mortgage expertise ranges from first-time homebuyers, repeat buying, luxury homes, refinancing, and building dream homes.

Frank attended Western Michigan University on a wrestling scholarship and graduated from Olivet College with a degree in business, where he played football and wrestled.

For more information about Frank Bennett, visit https://www.elementfunding.com/FBennett.

Buying and Selling Your Birmingham Home with a Specialist Agent Team

Josh Vernon and Jamey Reynolds

Introduction

Josh Vernon started his career in the banking industry. As a member of a local networking group, he frequently referred clients to another member who was a real estate agent. Josh observed the success of his real estate agent friend, and seeking a better opportunity, got his real estate license. While out with his wife on maternity leave, he decided to pursue real estate as a career. Within three years, Josh reached the top 1% among all real estate agents in the Birmingham area, and currently ranks among the top 200 agents in the country.

While working in sales at a retail flooring chain, Jamey Reynolds met Josh at an open house. Josh helped Jamey and his wife buy a home, and they became good friends. They began referring business to each other. Josh's success in real estate impressed Jamey, and with his ten years of sales experience, he decided to get into real estate with Josh as a buyer's agent in late 2013.

The Josh Vernon Group was created in 2014. Josh and Jamey are the team leaders, and they have a team of listing agents, buyer's agents, and administrative staff dedicated to providing excellent service to their clients. They help over 400 buyers and sellers each year with their real estate transactions.

In this chapter Josh and Jamey describe the development of their business model by incorporating a specialist real estate team concept and the benefits of their model for buyers and sellers in the Birmingham area.

Developing Our Specialist Team Concept

Josh sold 55 homes in his last full year working as an individual agent. With that individual transaction volume, it's challenging to stay on top of all that needs to be done simultaneously to move many transactions through the process to closing. When we started to work together as a team, we recognized the value of dividing our focus. In this way we could each specialize in different aspects of our business in order to deliver excellent service to our clients. Josh handled the listing side, helping sellers sell their homes. Jamey worked with buyers, helping them find and purchase homes.

Always striving to deliver the best experience for our clients, we reflected on our individual strengths and weaknesses, brainstorming ways to continually improve. We made a list of all the tasks a real estate agent must perform in their business. Most people would be amazed to know that an agent is responsible for almost 200 individual tasks from prospecting for clients to the closing. The list we use includes 184 specific tasks. A small sample of these tasks for a listing include the listing appointment, analysis of the market value, evaluation of the condition of the home, advise on pricing strategy, hanging a lockbox, installing a sign, ordering photography, production of flyers, posting the listing, and posting online listings. These are just a few of the tasks.

When an individual agent is handling all these tasks, it's like juggling a basketball, a bowling ball, a tennis ball, and a baseball all at the same time. They're all different weights and sizes. It's no wonder that the average real estate agent in the United States has only 7 to 9 transactions in a year. One of our observations was that both of us are better at client-facing, marketing-related, and problem-solving activities than with paperwork and administrative tasks.

Over a few short years we developed our specialist team concept to allow us to grow significantly while still delivering excellent service. We have unburdened our agents from administrative and repetitive tasks so they can focus on what they do best, help buyers find homes and help sellers sell their homes.

We have added agents and administrative personnel and we now have three divisions within our team, each focusing on specific areas of the business. Josh heads up our listing division which has a team of agents who focus on helping clients sell their homes. Jamey is responsible for our buying division with agents that help clients find and buy their ideal home. We also have a group of administrators who handle the paperwork and administrative tasks, like writing and adjusting contracts, ordering inspections, ordering title work, and making sure progress toward closing is on schedule. We even have a runner who hangs lockboxes, puts up signs, and delivers paperwork. With this structure, our agents are more available to provide valuable service to our clients, quickly answer phone calls, navigate through problems, and negotiate on behalf of our clients.

One of the most common complaints about real estate agents is a lack of communication, that leaves clients in the dark. When we begin working with clients, we try to learn their communication style. How do they prefer to handle communications? Do they prefer email, texts, or phone calls? What frequency do they prefer? Is it every day, every week, or only when there is something to report? While focusing their time on serving clients, our agents can trust the administrative team to handle the repetitive tasks, so they can provide the level of communications clients are seeking.

The structure we have developed has allowed us to handle around 400 transactions in a year. Our average agent transaction volume exceeds 30 transactions per year. This volume is providing our team over 40 times the annual experience of the average agent. Experience and learning are critical to continuously improving client outcomes and service levels. We have also been able to get the energy and synergy of an ongoing internal mastermind by sharing thoughts, ideas, experiences, what's working, and what's not working. While it's common in this industry to work in a reactive mode by putting out "fires," we strive to work in a proactive mode, preventing "fires" from even starting. We've tried to systematize our business so that those 184 different tasks are handled in the most effective manner possible to allow us to better serve our clients.

Real estate transactions require timely responses and action. On the other hand, life happens, and agents have their lives to live. They need to take vacations, go to the doctor, and attend school functions. Our structure provides backup so that if your agent needs some personal time, another agent will step in to make sure your home sale or purchase continues on the path to closing.

Most people preparing to buy or sell a home expect it to be a very stressful time and there can be obstacles along the way. Our philosophy is that buying or selling a home should be fun, and it can be when you are represented by an experienced agent or team that has your best interests at heart. As we've grown and developed our specialist team concept, we have adopted the slogan, "We make real estate fun."

Selling Your Home

Selling your home for the highest price generally requires some planning and preparation. We recommend that you contact a real estate agent as soon as you decide that you will be selling, no matter how far in advance. The sooner we can get started working with a seller, the better our ability to maximize the sales price and reduce the stress of selling. Timing the listing can influence the ultimate sales price. There are certain times of the year when fewer homes are typically on the market. During these times sellers may be able to get a higher sales price since there is reduced competition.

Everyone who sells a home has a unique situation. Consider your goals and objectives and make sure to communicate them to your real estate agent. We have an extensive checklist of questions we review during our first meeting with a seller. This helps our clients crystalize their goals and helps us fully understand what they are trying to achieve, so we can deliver the highest level of service.

Unfortunately, some people think they need to make a lot of changes prior to selling, and they begin improvements that may not bring a return on investment. An experienced agent can advise on the changes that will help sell your home for the most profit without spending a lot of money. During our initial meeting, we will make a detailed tour of your home, and work with you to develop a game plan for cost-effectively preparing your home for sale.

Accurate pricing to the market is very important for a fast sale and getting the highest price for your home. A common misconception is that pricing the home well above market value leaves room for negotiation, since buyers will try to negotiate the price down anyway. The other thought is that you can always reduce the price if it doesn't sell. There are several reasons why this is not a good strategy in today's environment. Buyers are generally searching for homes online, in well-defined price bands. If your home is overpriced, you may miss buyers looking for a home at your realistic market value. Most buyers set up alerts for new listings that match certain parameters. If they miss your home when it hits the market because it is outside their preferred price band, they probably won't see it if you reduce the price later. Buyers are well educated on values, especially when they are comparing your home to other similar homes for sale. If they come across an overpriced home, they will be less likely to set up a showing and the home may just sit on the market. Eventually the price needs to be reduced, and potential buyers wonder why the home has lingered on the market, leading to suspicions that something is wrong with the home. This just attracts low-ball offers. The solution is to price the home very close to estimated market value from the outset.

Along with setting a realistic price, exposing your home to the largest number of potential buyers is critical. Most buyers start their home search online, so an important factor is making your home stand out among the competition. As people are flipping through online listings, there are only a few moments to attract their attention, and compelling photos are the key getting your home noticed. Using a professional photographer makes a big difference in the quality of the photos. A professional will capture the home from the best angles and in the best lighting to make it stand out. Regardless of the price range of the home, we always hire a professional photographer to capture the best images that we will use online and in printed brochures.

Listings should be showcased on the real estate websites where buyers are looking. We invest in a number of online platforms for our listings and advertise to achieve premium placement on these sites so that our listings rank high when buyers are searching. We invest in capitalizing on each lead that views our online listings. We prefer inquiries coming directly to us so we can best represent our sellers. People spend time on social media, so we also feature our listings on Facebook and pay to boost the posts.

Even small details can help make your home stand out. As an example, we want our signs recognized as different from all the other ones in our market. We use a larger, professional looking sign with a 4x4 post. This costs a bit more, but it's our goal to turn something ordinary into the extraordinary.

The typical goal for sellers is to sell at the highest price and in the shortest amount of time. Our listing team is programmed to negotiate the highest and best price for sellers. The record for recent years is that our team has achieved an average selling price of around 99% of list price.

Buying Your Home

We talked earlier about how sellers should be as clear as possible in describing their goals in selling their home. It's no different for buyers, and we ask many questions during our first meeting with a buyer to get as much information as possible to define the characteristics of their ideal home. Location, size of home and lot, style, proximity to specific amenities, timing, and price point are some of the most important topics. We use a CRM (Customer Relationship Management) solution tailored specifically to the real estate industry to capture buyer preferences so we can establish search criteria for homes and provide alerts as soon as suitable homes that match the criteria go on the market. Our solution also automates follow-up reminders for our agents to communicate with our clients on the agreed schedule.

We recommend starting to work with a lender as soon as you are considering buying a home. If you need a loan to purchase a home, prequalification with a lender will give you peace of mind that you will be able to obtain a loan to purchase at the price point you are seeking.

A lender will give you information on different loan programs offered and how to balance down payment requirements with monthly payment obligations. For most people, the monthly budget for mortgage payments is important and a lender can help you work backwards from a monthly payment amount to a loan amount that will determine the price of home you can afford. If you don't make this determination before you are looking at specific homes, you could be wasting your time looking at homes that aren't in your budget. When you find the home you want to buy, you should already be able to provide prequalification for a mortgage because sellers typically do not respond to offers that are not backed up with a prequalification letter. If you wait until you find the ideal home, there's a good chance that another offer will be accepted before you are prequalified. If you don't already have a relationship with a lender, we can refer you to local lenders that are able to accurately underwrite loans and close on time.

Buyers are interested in saving as much money as possible when they are buying a home. The savings are not always just from reducing the purchase price. We have developed what we call our "bulletproof" contract form for buyers that can make hundreds or even thousands of dollars difference when buying a home. Our buyer's contract is more aggressive than the typical form used and requests the seller to pay most of the transaction expenses. We track savings achieved for our buyers compared to listing price. We break these down into categories like the price reduction itself, savings by getting the seller to cover typical buyer's transaction costs, and value of personal property negotiated to be included as part of the sale. We've maintained a track record of buyers paying an average of 95 to 96% of listing price or savings of approximately $7,500 each. This savings amounts to over 1.5 million dollars per year for our buyers.

Our bullet-proof contract also provides significant buyer protections in terms of establishing contingencies that must be met or else the buyer can walk away from the deal and receive the return of their earnest money on deposit. Typical contingencies relate to inspections, a home appraisal, and final approval of financing.

After you have identified the home you want to purchase and are under contract, our administrative team goes to work making sure all the detail tasks required to get to the closing are listed and then completed on time, making for a stress-free process. The administrator responsible for your contract will send an email listing all the tasks and who is responsible for ordering services and completing tasks for your closing. We have developed a list of qualified inspectors and other service providers that have proven to deliver high quality service in a timely and cost-effective manner.

The period from contract to closing can be a nervous time for everyone involved. The home or system inspections can uncover significant unseen problems which may require negotiations with the seller to remedy.

Sometimes problems are found with the foundation, roof, or HVAC system that a buyer doesn't want to deal with even if it can be repaired. In this case the buyer may just decide to walk away, as provided for in our contract. No house is going to be perfect, but an experienced agent can help you navigate through all the inspection findings, come to an informed conclusion, and make a decision on how to proceed. Our goal is to help our buyers find the right home for them, not in selling them a specific home.

Selecting the Right Agent

A home is the largest asset owned by most people, yet statistics have shown that the average person will spend more time shopping for appliances or TVs than in selecting a real estate agent to help them buy or sell a home. Considering the difference in value and the difference in experience level of real estate agents, it's hard to understand why more time isn't typically taken to choose an agent.

If you are considering an agent, whether referred by someone you know or that you have found in some other way, do some research to get an idea of the experience level. You can find information online about transaction volumes and we suggest you also look at reviews from past clients that are posted online. Experience and success level are highly related to transaction volume. While the average agent is involved in less than ten transactions in a year, more successful agents will have many times that level of transactions. Our team is helping hundreds of buyers and sellers every year.

It's a good idea to interview more than one agent before selecting one. Buying or selling a home can be a stressful time, and during the interviews you should get a sense that the agents know what they are doing and can guide you all the way through the process. If you don't get a good feeling about an agent, it's probably a sign that the agent isn't right for you. You'll be working closely with your agent and you should determine if their personality matches up with yours to make for the most enjoyable experience. With significant money at stake you should also feel comfortable that you can trust your agent to look out for your best interests.

If you are selling, ask to review examples of how the agent is marketing listings. Do they have the budget to spend on marketing to properly expose your home to the most buyers? What do they do in marketing that goes beyond what the typical agent is providing? Also ask for details of the percentage of average actual sale price to listing price.

Another important factor is the support team behind the agent. Does the agent have an assistant or other support staff to help with the administrative tasks? Does the agent have a backup plan to help you if the agent is on vacation or has personal business to attend to?

What Clients Are Saying

"I have had numerous transactions, buying and selling, with Josh Vernon and his team. Josh's team is cohesive and effortlessly works together to help you buy or sale your home. You always feel that you matter with Josh's group. Their responsiveness, knowledge of the Trussville market, professionalism, client satisfaction and team approach is hard to beat. We will not use another realtor other than Josh Vernon."

"We just closed on our first home with Jamey Reynolds and I'd have to say it went so smooth, I couldn't believe it! The whole team is just great, they make it as easy and stress free as possible for you. Buying your first home is always scary but having Jamey and his team really made it so exciting and enjoyable. I would definitely recommend them to any family and friends! I can't thank them enough!"

"Josh was phenomenal to work with, guiding us throughout the process of both selling and buying a home. After several past attempts at selling, we were fearful of getting yet another realtor and facing the disappointment of not being able to move, but he got it done. We love our new space and are forever grateful!"

"We were in the process of relocating for work to the Birmingham area when we met Jamey. He immediately put us at ease by action very listening to our situation, needs and desires for a home. By the end of the day we placed an offer on a home and Jamey went to work for us. He led the negotiations for the interior and exterior changes we desired, fending, deck, clean-up of brush, tree removal, getting quotes, and sending us pictures of the progress for the work.

It was as if we had a dedicated person working for us 120 miles away. And to top it off he is a person you immediately feel at ease with, like you have known him all your life. I recommend Jamey and the Josh Vernon Group without reserve!"

"The entire procedure was excellent! We were reluctant to use a real estate company to sale our home, but we were pleasantly surprised! Actually, it took all the worry and concern out of the picture. No better job could have been done. Thanks to the Josh Vernon Group."

"Couldn't have asked for a better realtor group! We are so happy in our new home. It was a low stress process. We are already enjoying our new home. Selling our house & moving into our new one was done in under a month! It was unreal. So thankful for this group!"

About Josh Vernon and Jamey Reynolds

Josh Vernon and Jamey Reynolds are co-owners of the Josh Vernon Group. They founded the Josh Vernon group in 2014 and they have consistently grown their business to become one of the largest teams in terms of transaction volume in the state of Alabama. They help buyers and sellers with their real estate transactions in the greater Birmingham area.

After ten years in the banking industry, Josh Vernon started his real estate career in 2010. He rapidly grew his business and within his first three years he reached the top 1% of all real estate professionals in the Birmingham area. Josh heads up the listing division which has a team of agents whose focus is helping clients sell their homes. He has won several awards for sales excellence including RE/MAX Hall of Fame, RE/MAX Platinum Club, and RE/MAX 100% Club.

Josh and his wife Natalie are raising three children in the Carrington Lakes Community of Trussville.

With ten years of sales experience in flooring, Jamey Reynolds started his real estate career in 2013. He heads up the buyer's division of the Josh Vernon Group with a team of agents that help clients find and buy their ideal home. Jamey is a graduate of Gadsden State Community College with an associate degree in Business and Marketing.

Jamey and his wife Arayah have a large extended family that they enjoy spending time with.

For more information about Josh Vernon and Jamey Reynolds, visit https://www.JoshVernonGroup.com.

The Right Mortgage for Your Home Purchase or Refinance

Brad Roche

Introduction

Brad Roche started in the mortgage industry while still in high school when he was an intern in his father's mortgage business in Michigan. He eventually took over responsibility for the business and established a presence in the Charlotte region in 2010. He has been a mortgage loan officer over the past twenty-five years, and has also been a licensed real estate agent, was a lead developer for commercial and residential property developments, and is a national mortgage industry coach and trainer. He is affiliated with Element Funding and is responsible for two offices in the greater Charlotte area.

Brad and his team help borrowers in North and South Carolina with their residential home purchase financing as well as refinancing. They offer a wide range of mortgage products including Conventional, FHA, VA,

Jumbo loans, and others.

In this chapter Brad describes how to obtain the right mortgage for purchasing of refinancing a residence.

Start Your Home Search with a Reliable Lender

The best way to start a home search is by talking with a lender that can evaluate your financial situation, review mortgage options that are available, and help you structure a loan that is affordable. We'll evaluate your income and assets and obtain a credit report during this initial process. The result will be a pre-qualification that indicates the amount of loan you can qualify for. It's not always just about the maximum loan amount you can qualify for because the size of monthly payment is a key part of everyone's budget. We can also work backwards with the desired monthly payment and down payment amount to arrive a loan size that will work within your budget. Once armed with a pre-qualification, you will know with a high level of confidence the price range of homes you can afford. It's really a waste of time to start shopping before knowing the price range you can afford.

I've observed that some people have been discouraged from even considering purchasing a home because they haven't saved up enough money for a down payment or they believe they won't be able to qualify for a loan. It's difficult to know for sure unless you speak with a loan officer who has access to a wide variety of loan programs. I have been able to help many clients over the years purchase a home with a very low down payment or even no down payment. It's a great feeling helping people achieve their dream of home ownership when they were initially discouraged from moving toward that dream.

There's another important reason to start the process with a lender. Most sellers insist that buyers show evidence of pre-qualification from a reliable lender prior to even considering an offer on their home. If you're not already pre-qualified when you find a home, you may lose the opportunity to other buyers that are prepared in advance.

All mortgage loan lenders are not alike. There are some national and online lenders that have a limited number of mortgage loan products available, but they are usually not the best fit for most borrowers. Most people are better served with a local lender that you can talk with on the phone or in person that will take the time to understand your situation and match you with a loan program that fits your financial objectives. Typically, large banks will have about ten different mortgage products available. That may work for most people, but there is usually not much flexibility. Mortgage bankers, like our firm, can offer a much broader range of mortgage products. As an example, we offer over fifty products, the same ones as the large banks, but also many more that may be better suited for our clients.

Look for a mortgage loan officer that has several years of experience and that can demonstrate a successful track record of loan volume as well as a high percentage of pre-qualified loans getting closed on time. Reviews and references from clients can be a good indicator of experience as well as client satisfaction.

Is the Lowest Advertised Interest Rate Loan the Most Affordable?

Lenders frequently advertise for borrowers by offering what are described as the lowest interest rates available. But are advertised rates always realistic and the most affordable option? The first thing to consider is that advertisements are used to attract consumers to start the conversation. Teaser rates are sometimes advertised that appear, on the surface, to be very low rates, but they may require a very large closing cost that needs to be paid to get the advertised low rate. The longer the term, generally the higher the rate, so some low rates advertised are for shorter loan terms, like a 15-year loan that will require higher monthly payments. Lower rates are not always better, and the best strategy is to look at the complete picture that includes not just the rate, but also the loan term, down payment requirement, closing costs, and monthly payments.

Most people are using cash for the down payment and they may also want to conserve money to buy furniture or make some improvements after purchasing a home.

The amount of closing costs frequently is an important consideration, so a loan with no closing costs can be attractive for most borrowers. I suggest reviewing the difference in interest rates and thus monthly payments between loans with and without closing costs. As an example, you might find that the lower interest rate loan requires $3,000 of closing costs, but the monthly payment is $40 less than a loan without closing costs.

Even without taking the value of money over time into account, it will take about six years of making the slightly higher monthly payments to equal the out-of-pocket closing costs on the lower interest rate loan. How long do you expect to live in the new home, and will you ever reach the break-even point? Younger families are more likely to move within five to seven years as they are growing their family size and may desire to move to a larger property or relocate for a new job.

This type of comparison also applies to people interested in refinancing. Over the past several years as interest rates were generally declining, we were able to help many clients refinance their fixed-rate loans, even two or three times, with no financed or out-of-pocket closing costs, lowering their monthly payments each time.

Everyone has different financial objectives and older couples that plan to live in the home over the long-term during retirement may be more interested in lower monthly payments. A discussion of both your short-term as well as long-term goals will help us tailor a mortgage program that works best for you.

Creativity in Structuring a Loan

Mortgage lenders typically offer a specific selection of mortgage products. Borrowers may or may not qualify for one or more of the products offered and the mortgages offered may or may not match with the borrower's objectives. What happens when a qualified borrower's objectives don't match with the programs offered? Unfortunately, with most lenders that's the end of the story.

I've learned over the years that, although the standard mortgage programs work for most borrowers, it's not always the case, and sometimes it takes out-of-the-box thinking to structure a loan program that will meet their financial objectives. I'll demonstrate with an example of a client's objectives that couldn't be resolved with a standard mortgage solution.

The client has excellent credit and a good income but doesn't want to put out a lot of cash for a down payment. The client wants to purchase a luxury home that costs about $600,000. The amount needed to be borrowed is larger than the limit on a conventional loan product that allows a small down payment. Most borrowers needing a larger loan than the conventional loan limit, would use a "jumbo" loan to finance their home purchase. The challenge with a jumbo loan is that a significant down payment is required. One solution we can offer for this borrower is a conventional loan at the maximum limit and a second mortgage for the balance. We can maintain the small down payment of the conventional financing and still get a great blended interest rate. While most lenders try to fit each borrower into a box, with our experience and wide variety of loan programs available, we can structure the loan to fit the client.

Overcoming the Mortgage Industry's Usual Complaints

Over the years, the number one complaint about the mortgage industry from clients and real estate agents is they don't feel like they are being kept well informed during the lending process. As you are selecting a lender, I'd recommend you inquire about how you will be kept updated on the status while your financing is being processed. Our team completely eliminated this complaint several years ago by developing a process to provide a weekly update every Tuesday by noon to our clients and their agents. Every client gets a Tuesday update in writing, so they know exactly where they are at in the lending process.

Getting from the purchase contract to closing is a very critical period for every real estate transaction. The buyer must navigate all the contingencies during what is called the "due diligence period," prior to closing a purchase. The buyer has put up a non-refundable deposit and all inspections, the home appraisal, and loan approval must be completed on the schedule agreed upon or the deposit may be forfeited. There is a large responsibility placed on the lender, getting the appraisal completed and the loan approved on time. This is a point of risk and you should get a good feeling when you select your lender that they will be able to get their end completed during the time allowed.

Another frequent complaint in the industry is that borrowers are surprised at closing with the amount of closing costs. When our clients are pre-approved, right upfront they are given a preliminary closing statement. It's not just an estimate; they receive a complete comparison in detail allowing adjustments to view 1 year, 5, 10, or any length of loan to see what the best match is for you. It's the same information they will see at closing, but they are better educated and confident on the decision. There has generally been improvement in regulations and compliance to limit the surprises at closing; however, we have gone beyond requirements by providing the exact cost information right up front. We also provide a sample closing package in advance of closing so the client can review the documents well in advance, so there are no surprises at the closing table.

Ten Things Not to Do That Can Delay Your Loan or Cause Possible Rejection

It's important to understand that your mortgage prequalification is based on the facts we have analyzed when completing the original underwriting for your loan. Changes to your credit or financial situation can affect the validity of the pre-qualification and can cause a possible rejection of your loan or delay your loan during the closing process, the most critical point in purchasing a home. I've listed below ten things not to do before closing on your new home and loan. If you feel that something on this list is necessary, be sure to check first with your loan officer.

1. Don't make large cash deposits to any of your bank accounts outside of normal payroll deposits. Sources of funds for a down payment must be tracked to authorized sources allowed under mortgage guidelines and cash going into your account is a red flag.
2. Don't open any new bank accounts.
3. Don't quit your job, change jobs, or become self-employed. Since your loan qualification is based on a stable income history, any change will jeopardize your loan.
4. Don't take any unpaid leave from your job. Unpaid leave will make your year-to-date income less than initially stated.
5. Don't spend money that has been set aside for closing costs or a down payment.
6. Don't use credit cards excessively. Also, don't let any accounts fall behind or increase credit limits.
7. Don't apply for any new credit accounts.

8. Don't buy furniture or appliances. You may want to get everything ready for your new home in advance but purchasing them should be delayed until after your loan is funded.
9. Don't buy a car, truck, van, or any other type of vehicle.
10. Don't co-sign a loan for anyone.

Value-Added Services for Our Clients and Business Partners

The majority of our business comes from repeat clients and referrals from our clients and business partners. We don't spend a lot of money on advertising and marketing, choosing instead to give back to our clients with programs that save them money and generate extra benefits that our competitors are not able to offer. Accurate pre-qualification for our clients is critical to eliminate surprises later in the process. We have invested in a local certified in-house underwriter to ensure that our loans go through properly. This pays off with an extremely high percentage of loans going through without a hitch after the pre-approval.

We have heroes in our community that put their lives on the line every day. These heroes include police officers, firemen, and military personnel. There are military veterans, many who have risked their lives for our country, that we help with VA loans. We also have essential service providers in our community including teachers and medical personnel. We consider all these people local heroes and we honor them by refunding a percentage of their closing costs when they obtain financing though us.

The Charlotte region is growing rapidly with companies and their employees relocating from all over the country. Families and individuals are also relocating here due to the growth in jobs and the quality of life. Relocations can be stressful, and we try to reduce the stress for relocating clients as much as possible. We've been licensed as a travel planners, so we can arrange flights, hotels, auto rentals, and restaurant reservations to make it easier for house-hunting trips to the area. We don't do this to make a profit, we do this to make our relocating clients time as efficient and stress free as possible and pass on the savings to our clients.

When we moved from Michigan to establish our first office in the Charlotte area, the country was in the middle of a major recession and we started building relationships in the community with local businesses. We built relationships with the Human Resources Managers of our business partners. Frequently when someone relocates to the Charlotte area for a job, the spouse needs to find a job in the local area as well. We use our connections with our many businesses partners to take the spouse's resume and promote employment within these businesses.

We initially offered to save these businesses' employees

money on their closing costs by being their preferred lender and the businesses reciprocated with benefits for all our clients - savings on their products and services. We have maintained these relationships over the years and our clients get an electronic package every quarter with product and service discounts from our business partners. All these extra benefits have grown over the years into what we call our "Passport to the Carolinas".

What Clients Are Saying

"Brad and his staff were very professional. They kept me abreast to every detail in purchasing my condominium. They got me an excellent interest rate too. They returned calls promptly. They made this huge event of purchasing a home on my own for the first time a Happy carefree time. I recommend Brad and his staff to you wholeheartedly."

--Susie

"Brad is incredible! He walked me through every question and concern that I had to assure my understanding, comfort and trust every step of the way! Brad also has an extensive knowledge and network of professionals to resolve the most challenging mortgage needs."

--Jeff

"Loved the Tuesday emails that kept me informed of what was needed from me and an update on where we were in the process.

I didn't have to worry about the details, because they guided me through the whole way."

--Christy

"We used Brad and his amazing team to assist in our new construction loan. They respond quickly to any questions. The team worked hard to meet all our needs. I would recommend Brad for any of your mortgage needs. This is our third time using his team and will never use anyone else."

--Karen

"Brad and his team made sure the process progressed fluently and kept me up to date weekly. Even after I was satisfied with a completed home purchased I received feedback. After 3 months of my home purchased I was advised that Brad and his team was able to drop the PMI on my mortgage. I will only recommend Brad and his team to my network of friends, family, and co-workers."

--Stuart

"A very well defined program that can handle any type of a tough loan issue and have just the right contacts or personal in the business for any situation ... from start to close they confirmed everything in terms that I understood.... and were patient and kind if i needed extra consolation on a topic or issue... Bottom line: I own because of them and would not have been able to without them... They can help you too."

--Shawn

About Brad Roche

Brad Roche is known among the Charlotte area real estate industry as "The Mortgage Planner." He is a mortgage banker and loan originator for Element Funding in Charlotte, North Carolina with two offices serving the greater Charlotte and Lake Norman areas. Brad has been a mortgage loan officer for over twenty-five years and consistently ranks in the Top 1% in the United States for loan originations, closing over 200 loans per year. He also was named among National Mortgage Professional Magazine's 40 Most Influential Mortgage Professionals Under 40 for 2015. He is a three-time bestselling author and has a weekly radio show that is broadcast in North and South Carolina by CBS, Fox, and ESPN where he provides insight on lending, real estate, and the plan to home ownership.

For more information about Brad Roche, visit https://www.BradRoche.info.

Buying or Selling Your Home in the Baltimore Area

Jason Perlow

Introduction

Jason Perlow grew up in the Baltimore area, and after graduating from the University of Delaware, he decided to pursue a career in real estate, a field where his mother had excelled for over two decades in the area. Jason has been licensed since 2011 and has built his real estate practice through his network of local businesses, other real estate agents and brokers, and hundreds of satisfied clients.

Jason is the team leader of the Perlow Home Team, affiliated with Berkshire Hathaway HomeServices Homesale Realty in Baltimore. He and his team help buyers and sellers in Baltimore, Baltimore County, and surrounding areas.

In this chapter, Jason provides insights for buyers and sellers in the greater Baltimore area.

Selling Your Baltimore Area Home

Objectives for Selling

With all the information available online today, many people planning to sell their home start their research on the Internet and ultimately get confused because there is lot of conflicting information about home values and how to sell a home. The best first step is to set up a consultation with one or more experienced real estate agents in your area. In my initial meeting with someone interested is selling their home, I'll ask several questions to make sure their objectives are clarified and there is an understanding on expectations. Why are they selling? When are they wanting to move? Do they have another home they are purchasing, or do we need to help them find a new house? Do they have a temporary rental lined up? Often, they haven't thought through these factors and the initial discussion helps bring clarity to their plan.

I'll walk through the home and provide some indications of things that should be done to get the home ready for sale and determine what kind of budget they have for preparing the home. We'll also discuss some preliminary information on the seller's expectations about pricing and how long it's likely to take for the home to sell.

Pricing

Expected selling price is almost always the biggest concern for the seller. We have a process to estimate market value that's very similar to what an appraiser goes through. We will find the most similar nearby homes that have sold in the prior six months and compare those homes to your home. Typically, we'll compare five homes. We'll also review homes in the local area that are currently on the market as well as homes under contract. One of the most important aspects of an accurate assessment is reviewing the details and photos of the homes we are comparing so we can note specific differences between homes that have sold and your home. In addition to number of rooms and square footage, even very similar homes can have different values based on location, condition, upgrades, and improvements. We also consider the market itself. What is the recent market trend? Are interest rates stable or changing? What time of year will the home go on the market? Armed with this information we present our estimated market value range to the seller. We'll also have pictures of the homes being compared to rationalize value differences.

Since valuation is not an exact science, I believe in establishing a price range rather than one specific price. The seller's needs will generally dictate the listing price. As an example, if a fast sale is needed to be able to close on another home, the home may be listed at the lower end of the range to precipitate a competitive environment to rapidly attract multiple buyers. If the seller is not in so much a rush, we may bring the home on the market slightly above the estimate range and there will be some room to negotiate if the buyer asks for some concessions, like closing costs. I'd recommend against an unrealistically high listing price as that's likely to result in fewer or no buyers showing an interest.

Preparation for Sale

Getting a home ready for sale is usually the most time-consuming part of the process. The more attractive you can make your home appear, the more interest you will have from buyers. I rarely recommend major improvements just before selling, such as changing appliances or redoing a kitchen, because it's difficult to get a good return on the investment. Even if you spent $20,000 redoing the kitchen, buyers may not appreciate the result and might rather make choices themselves. In general, we want to make the home look as clean and fresh as possible, so potential buyers can envision themselves living there.

Painting is the easiest way to freshen up a home. You should repaint walls that have bright, loud colors with neutral colors. There are some grey-tan shades that are currently popular. Repair any dings in the walls, ceilings, and trim. Make sure all fixtures and equipment are working properly and repair any loose handles on doors or cabinets.

One of the biggest mistakes we observe is not addressing stains from water leaks. You may have lived in your home for a long time and at some point, had a water leak or fixture overflow. Of course, we want to make sure any problems have been fixed, but you should also be sure to patch or paint any areas that are stained, a big red flag for buyers walking through your home.

Removal of clutter around the home is a very important step in getting your home ready. We have a team member that will walk through your home and make a list for you of things that should be removed or rearranged. Countertops and shelving should be cleared of all but essential items. Most of the pictures and artwork should be removed from the walls. We may also recommend rearranging or removing some of the furniture to create a more open and spacious appearance.

When buyers come by to look at your home, first impressions are made as they are getting out of the car and walking up to the front door. The landscaping should be tidy and well maintained. Power wash the driveway and walks. Depending upon the season, a few flowers in bloom and fresh mulch will make a nice statement. Look around the exterior for signs of wood rot and repair any issues. Paint may need to be touched up and a power washing of the exterior will remove dirt and stains. The front porch should be clean, and a new mat will be welcoming to visitors.

Marketing That Works to Sell Your Home

Although we still do print advertising in upscale magazines and use a variety of media to showcase our listings, technology has changed to the point where most buyers are looking at homes on the Internet. Our listings go on the Multiple Listing Service and are syndicated to key real estate websites like Zillow and Trulia and then to thousands of other sites where people look for homes.

The most important day for selling your home is the day we bring in a professional photographer to capture the home's beauty. With short attention spans, we only have few seconds to capture buyers' attention and high definition quality photos are absolutely necessary. Even if the home is exceptional, unless the photos pop online, most buyers aren't going to be interested in a showing. If the home is in a nice setting, we also like to use aerial drone photography so people can see what the view and neighborhood looks like. We also incorporate 3D virtual tours, a tool buyers can use to go through the home room-by-room while looking at the online listing.

It takes a lot more than just listing your home for it to sell. Our team uses several proactive approaches to generate buzz and get wider exposure. Right before the home listing goes live, we like to use a feature called "Coming Soon," that is available on certain real estate websites. We may be in the final preparation stage and don't want buyer showings yet, but we announce the upcoming listing this way to start attracting attention and lets buyers and their agents know when it will be available for a showing. Not only do we use open houses to attract byers, we often schedule broker open house events on Wednesdays to get other agents who may have clients for our listing to come and take a look.

Sometimes neighbors can be good sources of buyers from people they know that want to move into the same neighborhood. We mail "Just Listed" postcards to about 150 neighbors in the immediate surrounding community. We also send out Virtual eCards describing our listings to our network of other agents and brokers in the area. People are hanging out on social media platforms like Facebook and Instagram, so we feature our listings and announce open houses there as well.

Showings

Our pre-marketing and marketing efforts usually start driving buyers to look at the home soon after listing. You will get notice of a requested showing, but sometimes it is on very short notice. It's critical to keep the home clean and neat during this period, so it can be shown at any time. Buyers will recognize that the home is being lived in, but everyday items shouldn't be left lying around. Make sure that the beds are made, dirty clothes are put into a hamper, and dirty dishes aren't left in the sink. If you have a pet, pet hairs and other evidence of a pet should be removed. Odors from pets and cooking are another problem, so pay attention to things like this that can make your home unappealing to many buyers.

We use a showing service to schedule our showings. I get a notification about a requested showing and contact the seller to verify if the schedule works. Some of our clients who always have a cell phone with them decide to receive showing requests directly by text message and they can respond with a text message back. Some buyers have a limited time to look at homes, so it's better to accommodate them with a showing at their preferred time.

Negotiating the Offer

All offers are not the same and they can vary in several ways. The most obvious point is the price, but there are other elements that can be critically important to the seller as well. An all cash offer is great, but most home purchases require mortgage financing. We always make sure that prospective buyers present a credible preapproval letter from a reliable lender along with their offer. Each type of loan has advantages and disadvantages for the seller. You will find that offers will also differ on the proposed time to settle, or close, the transaction. One buyer may offer a higher price but needs 75 days to close while another with a lower price can close within 30 days. Does the seller need a relatively fast closing in order to purchase another property or for another reason or is timing less important? Virtually all offers provide for some contingencies, the most typical ones being satisfactory inspections and financing/ appraisal approval. How much time is being requested to remove contingencies? Some buyers may request a contingency related to selling their own home. That can be a particularly risky one for a seller to accept since the seller has no control over the sale of the buyer's home. Whether you have one offer to consider or multiple offers, we will analyze the pros and cons of each offer and help you make the most informed decision on ranking the offers in order of favorability. Most of the time we will also advise on a counteroffer and help the seller negotiate the best final deal.

Buying Your Baltimore Area Home

<u>The Best Way to Get Started</u>

Often, people interested in buying a home start their search online and begin browsing houses in many areas and at different price points. You can get feel for what homes are selling for, but it's usually not productive to shop before knowing for sure what you can afford. You might like homes you see selling for over $400,000, but if you discover later that you will only be able to purchase a $250,000 home your dreams may be shattered. On the other hand, you may think you can only qualify for a home at a lower price than you really want and that would be a better fit for your family. You may find that you can qualify for a higher price home than you thought.

The very best way to start your home search is to get prequalified with a mortgage lender. During my first meeting with homebuyers, I always check whether they have started working with a lender. If not, I can connect them with lenders that offer a variety of loan programs. The lender will review your financial information, run a credit check, advise on mortgage options available, let you know how large a mortgage you can qualify for, and how much the corresponding monthly payments will be. They will also issue a preapproval letter that provides a level of confidence to you and sellers that that you will be able to close on the financing. Even if you qualify for a certain amount of loan, you may not feel your budget will allow the monthly payments for the maximum loan. Your lender will be able to help you work backwards to determine the price of a home you can both qualify for and still be within your monthly payment budget.

During our first meeting we will also explore what buyers are looking for in a new home. Lifestyle and stage in life play a big part in determining both locations that might work as well as types of properties that are best suited to them. How large of home are they looking for? What kind of lot? Some people, especially if they are already living in the Baltimore area, know where they want to live, and others look for some advice based on their lifestyle preferences. We'll explore what types of nearby amenities they prefer, such as parks, shopping, restaurants, or nightlife. If they have children, proximity to top rated schools are usually important. Are there certain activities that their children enjoy, making proximity a priority? Are they interested in city life or more suburban living? Once we know their budget and interests, we can generally narrow down to a small number of zip codes that most likely will match their needs. This will help to identify specific properties and we can start scheduling showings for our clients.

Some people starting their home search may think they

don't need their own agent. Most properties for sale can be seen online, so it may seem like buyers can just call up the listing agents to see the homes and work directly with the listing agents. Although that is possible, the real issue is representation. The seller's agent has a fiduciary responsibility to the seller, so buyers are on their own in this scenario with respect to true evaluation of the price, negotiations, interpreting inspections, and all other matters. The seller's agent is also not going to suggest other properties that may be appropriate for you. The cost to use a buyer's agent is borne by the seller as part of the selling agent's commission, so there is not a cost to the buyer to use a buyer's agent who will look after the buyer's best interests throughout the process.

Structuring an Offer

Once you have visited a selection of available homes, there are probably some that stand out as the best matches and that you want to revisit before making an offer. Pricing is one of the main elements of an offer, so we will analyze the market value of one or more homes that you are interested in to provide insight on a fair offer price. Our analysis is like the one we would perform for a seller, where we compare the most comparable nearby homes that have sold in the prior six months and make valuation adjustments for the differences. We will also advise on the current market conditions and expectations for level of competition from other buyers. We'll look at how long the house has been on the market and how many other homes are for sale to estimate the competitive situation. If the seller has already moved and the home is vacant, that can be an indicator of a more flexible seller because there may be payments being made on two houses. We'll also look at the condition of the home, if it is older. For example, if it appears that something major like the roof or HVAC system will need to be replaced soon, and that doesn't seem to be considered in the list price, we'll advise on an appropriate adjustment to the price. You may also want to request help with paying closing costs especially where you must pay for specialized inspections that can be expensive.

The more we can learn about the seller's situation, the better chance we have of crafting an offer that will stand out. It's not always just about the price. I contact the seller's agent to get as much information as possible about when they need to settle and anything else related to preferred timing of the transaction. Sometimes a quick closing is desired so another home can be purchased. Other times, the seller may desire to hold off closing until another home is completed. Sometimes a short rent-back is preferred. Depending on the buyer's flexibility, we can try to structure an offer that benefits the seller in terms other than just the price and may be able to get our offer considered above others even with a lower price.

Getting to the Closing

After the offer is negotiated and a purchase contract

is signed, there are still some important steps to get to the settlement. The purchase contract will provide for contingencies that will allow you to back out and receive your earnest money deposit back if the contingencies are not satisfied. Time is of the essence, so you will need to make sure you adhere to the schedule or you can jeopardize your deposit.

One of the key contingencies is for a home inspection and possibly other specialized inspections to make sure the home and its systems are in good condition. We generally have a normal home inspection and a termite inspection. We recommend a radon inspection as well in this area. Many homes outside the cities in Baltimore County are served with a private well and septic system. These systems should always be inspected and tested. If the home inspection findings show a problem with a roof or heating and air conditioning, we may recommend having a specialist check as well. We have a list of inspection services we can recommend that have a history of doing quality work and working within the time constraints called for in the contract. Inspections cost money, but a buyer is much better off knowing the issues when you can still negotiate a satisfactory resolution. You don't want to buy the house with major issues and not find out until after you have moved in. We negotiate on your behalf to either get the seller to remedy the issues or provide a credit so that you handle repairs. Most of the time we come to an agreement that is satisfactory to both sides, but if it can't be resolved, the buyer can back out and get a return of the earnest money deposit.

Unless you are paying with cash, another contingency will be related to getting your mortgage approved by certain date. Your lender will require an appraisal and it will need to show the value at or above the purchase price. Again, it's important to stay within the time frame provided in the agreement.

Selecting the Best Agent for You

With so many real estate agents, how do you know which one is right for you? Whether buying or selling, experience is a key factor. It not just years of experience, but volume of successfully completed transactions that should be considered. You can get a view of volume on some real estate sites. Reviews are another good indicator. Lots of good reviews indicate not just volume, but satisfied clients. You can also ask for references from past clients to get a deeper understanding of how an agent has served them. Sites like Zillow and Realtor. com show maps with locations of an agent's activity. Real estate is a local market and you will be best served by selecting an agent that has been active in the area where you are selling or are interested in buying a home.

When talking with an agent, I suggest you inquire about availability. Does the agent work full time? Is the agent available in the evenings or weekends? If you are buying and an attractive new listing pops up, you can lose the opportunity to buy it if your agent isn't able help set up a showing and follow through with writing an offer.

If you are selling, check out how the agent has been marketing listings. Do the photos look professional and make the home stand out? Does the agent create nice brochures? Look at examples of Internet, social media, and print advertising. The other thing to consider is how the agent communicates their view on valuation. Does the agent just take a listing for what you think it is worth, or does the agent do a market analysis and provide evidence of market value, even if it doesn't agree with your expectations? Our team doesn't just list homes, we sell homes.

Does the agent have support to help clients all through the process? Some agents work independently and don't have a backup plan for clients when they are busy. We've found that a team approach works best. We have specialists that work on the listing and buying side and have the resources within our team to deliver a high level of service even when one team member needs to take some personal time or is on vacation.

What Clients Are Saying

"Jason and his team were an absolute joy to work with. We used Jason in both the buying and selling of our home in Baltimore and would easily recommend him to anyone who asks. When buying, my wife and I looked at quite a few homes and Jason was always prompt to get us a showing and knowledgeable about each home and the surrounding area. Once we found the right home he made the buying process incredibly fast and easy. He was always prepared with answers for my many questions, and made something so stressful seem very manageable. Selling the home with Jason was also a breeze. I felt like he had our best interests in mind and because of his professionalism and preparedness had the house sold a few days after hitting the market. Anytime someone asks for a recommendation we always throw them Jason's way."

"They were thorough, and excellent, Jason made a lot of good recommendations. The whole process was done very professionally. I couldn't have asked for a better process start to finish. Best realtor I've worked with by a mile!"

"My husband and I thought that Jason and his associate, Rachael, were fantastic! They were professional, responsive, attentive, knowledgeable -- everything you would want in your realtors. They worked together to arrange photos, help us stage the house, come up with an appropriate price, advertise, show the house, arrange inspections, negotiate with the buyer, and close. They did a great job! Our house was on the market for only 2 weeks and we didn't even need to have a public open house. We would recommend Jason and Rachael very highly"

"Jason was our realtor in the sale of our home and we couldn't have been happier with him. As first time sellers, we had a lot of questions and Jason was incredibly responsive in answering all of them. He's extremely knowledgeable about the Baltimore area and offers excellent insight into the local market."

"Working with Jason, we were able to get our house under contract in under a week! We can not recommend Jason highly enough! Working with him in the sale of our home was a pleasure."

"An incredible experience! Professional, knowledgeable and fast! Sold our house at the right price in less than a week. Understood the needs of both sides of the transaction(s). Could not have asked for more."

About Jason Perlow

Jason Perlow is the team leader of the Perlow Home Team and is affiliated with Berkshire Hathaway HomeServices Homesale Realty in Baltimore, Maryland. He and his team help buyers and sellers with their residential real estate transaction in Baltimore, Baltimore County, and surrounding areas.

Jason is a graduate of the University of Delaware and has been a licensed real estate agent since 2011. He has been recognized for sales excellence in real estate, including being recognized by Real Trends as among the top 1% of all agents in sales volume in America and the Chairman's Gold Club of the Number 1 real estate producing company in the Baltimore region.

Jason has appeared on the nationally televised HGTV series, "Househunters Revolution." He also believes in giving back to the local community. He has served as a mentor with the Greater Chesapeake Big Brothers Foundation, is a current board member of the Nikki Perlow Foundation, and has been honored as one of "Maryland's Finest" sponsored by the Cystic Fibrosis Foundation.

For more information about Jason Perlow, visit http://www.PerlowHomeTeam.com.

Relocating to the North Dallas Area

Troy Olson

Introduction

Troy Olson started his real estate career in Scottsdale, Arizona after he realized there must be a better way to buy a home after a bad experience with a real estate agent representing a seller while trying to buy his first home in area. He decided to get his license and represent himself to purchase a home. Troy rapidly discovered that average real estate agents didn't have the knowledge to deliver the experience buyers and sellers expected when buying or selling a home, which is a usually their most valuable asset. Troy started to focus on his real estate career in 2004 in the Phoenix area and moved to the Dallas area in 2005.

Troy and his team help buyers and sellers with their home purchase and sale transactions in the North Dallas suburbs. His specialty is helping relocating buyers find their dream home in the North Dallas area.

In this chapter Troy Olson provides insights for buyers relocating into the North Dallas area.

Why People Are Moving to the North Dallas Suburbs

The greater Dallas-Fort Worth Metroplex is a very attractive area to live in for a variety of reasons and we have seen tremendous growth in the North Dallas area for several years. The suburbs of Frisco and McKinney have been among the fastest growing cities in the country. Overall cost of living is reasonable, and housing is very affordable compared to most large metro areas of the United States. Job growth in the area, fueled by corporate headquarters and large office relocations, has led to a great job market and low unemployment rates. There are no state income taxes in Texas, and that fact provides a big financial incentive for people to relocate from some of the high tax states on the coasts. Our school systems in the northern suburbs have a great reputation, another reason for families wanting to live here.

Texas has a favorable business climate which is driving company relocations and expansions to the Dallas-Fort Worth area and several other cities in the state. Just like for individuals, there are no state corporate income taxes in Texas. The state and municipalities have several programs to attract business and significant financial incentives are offered to relocating companies that promise to add jobs in the area. Even with low unemployment rates, people moving into the area in large numbers increase the available workforce. DFW Airport is a major transportation hub and almost any city in the country can be reached within three hours.

Many large companies have established operations in the boundary between Plano and Frisco. One of the larger relocations was the move of Toyota's North America Headquarters from California. Liberty Mutual Insurance, State Farm Insurance, and Chase Bank have all built large campuses in the area. Raytheon has large operations here as well. The PGA of America is moving their headquarters to Frisco from Florida and Uber is developing a major hub in Dallas.

First Steps in Finding Your New Home in the Area

People moving to the North Dallas area may have some knowledge about the area, but they almost always can benefit from some discussion about their objectives and review of alternatives that will best match their needs. In my first call or meeting with prospective homebuyers I try to gather as much information as possible about what they are looking for in a home and neighborhood. It's more than just about the specifics of the house they are looking for, like the square footage, number of bedrooms and bathrooms, lot size, and number of parking spaces in the garage. What else is important to them? Families with children are going to be interested in school system rankings. Commute time to work is a common concern. But what about the desired lifestyle and the activities that are important to the family? Some families are interested in a community swimming pool that their children can enjoy but may not want to maintain their own pools. Are there sports or other activities your children are interested in? I've had clients that had horses and they needed a solution for boarding, which influenced locations that would work for them.

Most homebuyers are initially focused on the characteristics of the home, but I've found that by taking a comprehensive approach to discovering a family's needs and wants, they can achieve a better outcome and find the home that will be the most satisfying to them for several years.

Establishing a budget for a home is another important point before we start looking at homes. I always advise buyers to get a preapproval letter from a local lender with a good reputation at the beginning of the home search. Going through this process will provide a high level of confidence on the amount of loan you will be qualified for as well as the amount of the monthly payments. You may also want to work backwards from a comfortable payment along with a down payment amount to see the loan amount and thus price of a home that will work for your budget. Getting this clarified upfront eliminates wasted time. You don't want to be out looking at homes that cost $600,000 if your budget or financing capability suggests you should be buying a home that costs $400,000.

Another important reason to get preapproved upfront is that sellers and their agents won't even consider offers on a home unless they are accompanied by a preapproval letter from a reliable lender. If you wait to start working with a lender until you find a home you want to purchase, you may find that someone else who was better prepared makes an offer and gets the home before you are ready. Shopping for a home without preapproval is like going to the store to shop without your wallet.

Working with a Buyer's Agent

Most homes for sale are listed online which leads some people to believe they can just contact the listing agents to see homes they may be interested in considering. Of course, this is possible, but it's almost always the worst choice for a homebuyer. Listing agents are contractually obligated to represent the seller, and part of that representation is to try to make the most money for the seller in the transaction. A buyer's agent represents the buyer, helps the buyer make the best deal on a home, and helps navigate through the transaction all the way to closing. Having your own agent benefits in several ways. Without a buyer's agent you are on your own in identifying properties that may match your requirements, and I've found that most clients I help miss several ideal properties by looking online by themselves. Experienced agents are experts in their field and can interpret the various disclosures and documents involved in the transaction. It doesn't cost the buyer anything to engage a buyer's agent as the seller pays the commission on both sides of the sale, and it is the same regardless if the listing agent handles both sides or there is an agent involved on each side.

Identifying Potential Homes to Purchase

Once we have a good understanding of your budget and wants and needs in a home, we set up a search portal that will identify listings that meet your criteria. It's like a search engine to help prepare for a home search visit to the area. We also independently compile a catalog of listings that meet your criteria that we can visit with you. When you are here in the area, we will take a tour of the different towns, developments, and neighborhoods that match your criteria so you can get a good idea of what each area looks like and what each area has to offer. I always suggest driving around with a purpose, not just driving around on your own trying to figure it all out. We want to get you inside homes in each area so you can get more than just a look at different areas. You also get a better feel of what your money can buy and it's important to know that pictures you see online can be deceiving, so it's better to be able to see inside homes as we tour the area.

As I mentioned, commute times are important for most people. During their decision-making process, some clients make a trial drive during typical morning commute times to see how long it takes to drive to work from different locations. This can be different than driving in the middle of the day or over the weekend.

Master Planned Communities in the North Dallas Suburbs

Some very unique master planned communities have been developed in our North Dallas suburbs in recent years that are attracting a lot of families moving into the area. These developments all have a wide variety of amenities and an activity schedule so that residents don't really have to drive a distance to participate in a variety of sports and other activities. It's almost like living at a resort or private club. Each development has a Homeowners Association (HOA) that maintains the amenities as well as front yard maintenance for the residents.

The Windsong Ranch development consists of over 2,000 acres in the town of Prosper. Over 600 acres are devoted to green space, parks, trails, and amenities. One elementary school is located within the community and another elementary school, a middle school, and a high school are planned to be built, all within the preferred Prosper Independent School District (ISD). The community will ultimately include 3,500 homes and four unique amenity centers. Amenities include a resort-style pool, a 5-acre clear tropical lagoon with a beach, tennis courts, and a fitness center, along with parks and trails. A 46-acre retail center is also part of the development.

Light Farms in Celina is another local master-planned development. This community consists of over 1000 acres and more than 240 acres are reserved for green space, playgrounds, parks, greenbelts, and a community lawn. The development is within the boundary of the award-winning Prosper ISD and four schools are located within the development. Amenities at Light Farms include over 13 miles of trails, 5 pools, tennis courts, a fitness center, and more. A retail center is also planned as part of the community.

Mustang Lakes is another master-planned community in Celina. The development includes over 60 acres devoted to open space and 8 lakes are on the site. Students attend schools in the Prosper ISD and an elementary school is planned within the development. This community has a large amenity center, resort-style pool, fitness center, 10 miles of trails, and a 5-acre stocked lake.

Making an Offer

After looking at homes and deciding on one you are interested in purchasing, it's time to consider an offer. We'll look at the seller's disclosures and run comps to see if the price is in line with a realistic market value.

Depending on our assessment of market value relative to the listing price and prevailing market conditions, there may be a competition among buyers to purchase the home and multiple offers may be submitted. This will influence how our offer is developed to have the best opportunity to be considered. We'll try to determine other terms that may be important to the seller. Sometimes we discover that the seller has certain unspoken objectives that we can address in the offer to make it more attractive. One example is a desire to rent back the property for a few weeks after the closing so the seller can have time to purchase another property. With an understanding of what the seller is looking for we can craft an offer that is responsive to the seller's needs while still making a good deal for the buyer. Sometimes there is an opportunity to include personal property like a washer, dryer, refrigerator, pool table, or media room equipment into the sale and these points need to be negotiated. Typically, after the offer is submitted there will be some additional negotiations before the purchase contract is signed by both parties.

Getting to the Closing

Our standard purchase contract form in Texas for resale properties provides for an option period for the buyer to exit the contract. The option period is usually between seven to ten days and during this time the buyer can hire a home inspector to evaluate the property and provide an inspection report with findings. Sometimes issues are discovered that suggest another inspection by a roofing, HVAC, plumbing, or an electrical inspector for further review. Hailstorms are common here, so we frequently get a roofer or even an insurance company to review the roof to make sure the roof is in good condition and is insurable. Depending on the inspection findings, this can result in additional negotiations to repair certain issues that were discovered by the inspector. If agreement cannot be reached on resolution, the buyer can terminate the contract during the option period.

Generally, the purchase contract provides a contingency for the home appraising for a value at or above the purchase price. In times of tight inventory and when homes are attracting multiple offers above the listing price, this can present an additional issue. Appraisals are opinions of value and there are times that the appraisal doesn't come in at the price negotiated in the contract. This is another point that may necessitate another round of negotiations to resolve.

Selecting an Agent

Not all real estate agents are the same and the best outcome usually follows selecting an agent with a high level of experience in the local market where you are interested in purchasing. Look for an agent that specializes in the specific area where you are interested in purchasing a home. The Dallas-Fort Worth Metroplex covers an area of over 11,000 square miles and agents can't really have detailed knowledge throughout the entire metro area. Reviews are a good indicator of expertise and if you search for reviews on specific agents you can see several sites that provide published reviews. Volume of successful closed transactions is another indicator of success that you can research online.

Helping clients find their dream home is a time-consuming activity and the best results are achieved when working with an agent that has the time to focus on satisfying your needs. I suggest you consider agents that have a team behind them that can provide backup to provide support all throughout the home purchase process.

What Clients Are Saying

"Troy Olson is the hardest working agent I have ever dealt with whether buying or selling. I had my real estate license for 7 years in the state of Colorado and I would not have wanted to compete with Troy. He is the only agent I will recommend to my friends. I currently have relatives and friends that have real estate licenses and as much as I like them, they do not have the work ethic that Troy has. Troy was responsive any time of the day or evening."

"I rated Troy at the top of each survey question for a reason - he deserved it. If I had to choose a couple of attributes above the rest, I'd say his trust and timely communications are stand-outs. He understands the fast pace of the North Dallas housing market and used his incredible work ethic to respond quickly to push our deal (offers & response) through in a timely manner. Many times we'd ask Troy his opinion of a home we were toured -- he did not waver with providing us with his honest opinion about location, marketability, concerns, etc. It's easy to understand why we trusted him so much. This was key for our home search & purchase."

"We have just closed on our new house in Frisco, TX, and highly recommend Troy and his entire team. He is super knowledgeable about the different communities, and is able to help target the neighborhoods and developments that make the most sense for each buyer. Troy was super responsive from day one. He asked the right questions, was very thorough with his follow-up, and ensured our closing was smooth and painless. We highly recommend Troy and his entire team."

"Troy and his team made this extremely daunting task of searching and buying a house in TX so much easier for us. He and his team made sure to answer every question, address every request extremely promptly. He guided us along the entire process with his valuable experience and knowledge of the market there and was extremely accommodating for every situation. His services did not end just with the closing of our house. He continues to help us in every possible way as we prepare to transition to the new location. I have and would continue to recommend him to everyone who is looking for a home in TX."

"The Troy Olson Team truly cared about me and my move. They updated me throughout the entire process and with their work ethic, I could relax and not have to worry about the all the details. Buying and selling homes is already stressful enough to not have a great team to support and guide you through the process. The Troy Olson Team are Rock Stars!"

"Troy is incredible knowledgeable about the area & the market. He always went above & beyond to be available and ensure that we had everything we needed to make a decision. We had three days to buy a house and Troy made that experience much less stressful than we ever thought it would be. We recommend his team to everyone we know! You won't be disappointed!"

About Troy Olson

Troy Olson and his team help buyers and sellers with their home purchase and sale transactions in the North Dallas area. His specialty is helping companies and their employees relocating to the North Dallas area.

For more information about Troy Olson, visit https://www.TroyOlsonTeam.com.